Offa's Dyke
In the time of Covid

Stephen Platt

www.leveretpublishing.com

Offa's Dyke: In the time of Covid
First published - August 2022
Published by Leveret Publishing
56 Covent Garden, Cambridge, CB1 2HR, UK

Hay Bluff, Pen y Begwn (677)

ISBN 978-1-912460-51-9

© Stephen Platt 2022

All rights reserved. No part of this publication may be reproduced, stored in a retrieval system or transmitted in any form by any means, electronic, mechanical, photocopying, recording or otherwise, except brief extracts for the purpose of review, without the written permission of the publisher.

Offa's Dyke
In the time of Covid

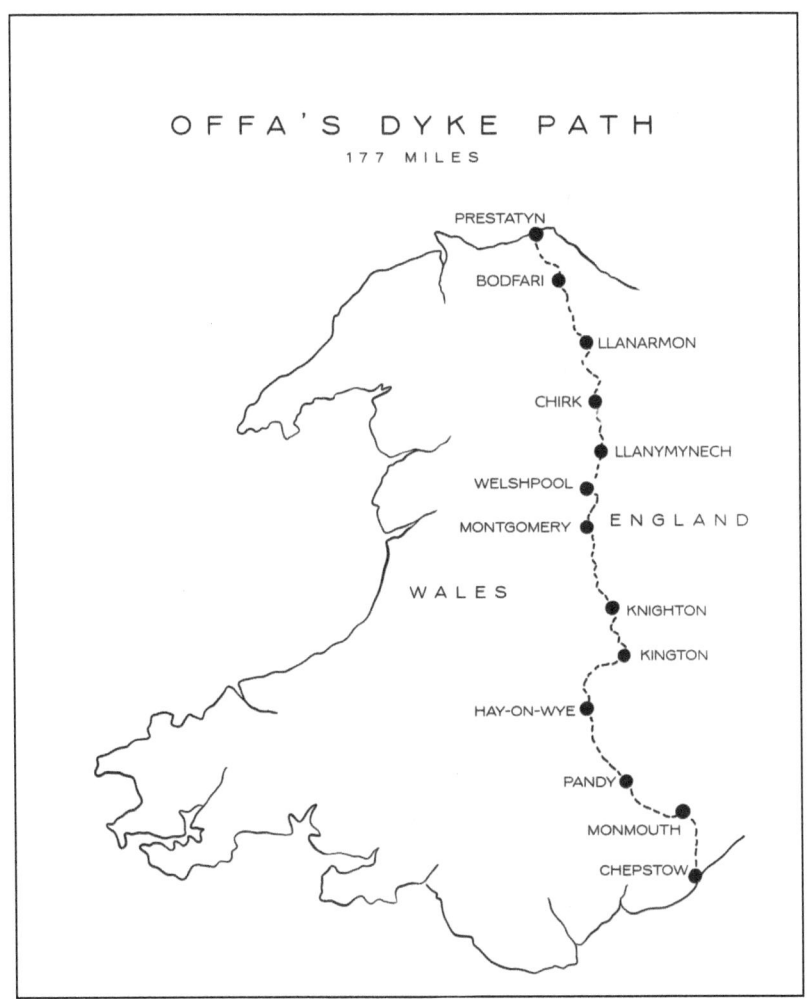

Day 1 Train to Chepstow; Walk to Sedbury and back

Sunday 12 June (4 miles)

I am doing Offa's Dyke differently to how I did the Coast-to-Coast last year and the Pennine Way the year before. This time I'm staying in hotels rather than wild camping, and I'm going by train instead of by car. The weather looks fine, I've a light pack and I'm ready for off and looking forward to the trip. I went to the Black Mountains, in the southern part of the walk, when I was learning to hang-glide off Hay Bluff with Scharlie in the 80s, and I remember rock climbing near World's End in the Clwydian range while at University in the 60s. But there are long stretches that are new to me. I'm on a mission to explore new places; to get away from the crowds on the beaten tracks of Snowdonia, the Peak, and the Lakes, that I know so well, and immerse myself in the less well-known places that attract less people. I also want to get a feel for the place, its geology, its history, how people lived in the past and how the economy works

Hathersage railway station

today. It will help me take stock of where we are in Britain today and what hope there is for the future.

I have been reading English Pastoral by James Rebanks, in which he recounts his upbringing on a Lake District fell farm. He describes what he learned from his grandfather about farming with nature, and how he took on the yoke of the farm when his father died. It's what Scharlie has been doing in a small way at Leveret Croft. At first sight this is nothing to do with Offa's Dyke, but one of the things I've been doing on these long walks is taking stock, noticing what is happening in the countryside and relating this to what I've been reading and what Scharlie has been telling me. I've noticed the wildflower borders at Hathersage Station and the Yellow Rattle and weeds between the tracks at Sheffield station. Many of the fields we pass in the floodplain of the River Severn are lying fallow. They look as though they are grazed and planted on rotation and there are many copses and hedgerows.

I get a coffee in Gloucester and then it's only a short hop to Chepstow. On the walk up the hill from the station there is the sound of jazz played by a guy on the corner in front of the Cenotaph on Bank Street. There is a covered market and I find Gregg's and buy a pasty and go and eat it sitting on the Cenotaph steps. It's relaxing listening to the music and watching passers-by.

Chepstow Bank Street

> **Chepstow, Cas-gwent (12,000)**
>
> There has been continuous human occupation on or near this site since 5000BC. Chepstow Castle was built in 1067, immediately after the Norman Conquest, on a cliff above the crossing of the River Wye and is the oldest surviving stone castle in Britain. Chepstow was given its first charter in 1524, flourished as a major port, and reached its peak during the Napoleonic Wars. Today it's a thriving local market town and tourist destination.

After half an hour I galvanise myself and head off to start the walk in Sedbury. The weather is nice, and I have plenty of time. There are new flats below the road bridge over the River Wye and a builders' dump; maybe they're planning more development. I weigh up the tide line on the limestone cliffs on the opposite bank and wonder if they might flood with sea level rise. The path winds through bungalows of new homes with clip-on Georgian front doors. The verge has been left unmown and a sign, rather the like the one Scharlie's rewilding group placed on Jagger's Lane, that explains they are leaving the grass unmown for bees and other pollinators. The path is mean – squeezed

Chepstow and Castle

between fences between housing and the river. It would be a bit depressing if it weren't such a beautiful day.

Beyond the sandstone cliffs that border the river there is a seagrass margin and mudflats. I leave my pack leaning against a log and strike out for the water's edge but am balked by claggy mud and retreat and contemplate the silvery water and the Severn Crossing bridge.

On the way back, I'm accompanied by the chatter of house sparrows and a man burning the weeds on the path in front of his house with an electric gun; it looks more trouble than it's worth. Crossing the bridge I survey the building rubble on the building site below the bridge – stone and plastic piping, insulation rolls and Kingspan, oil tanks and toilet bowls, wheelie bins and bricks. What a mess. Someone has built a den using sheets of steel reinforcing mesh for the walls and slats for the roof. There are two armchairs. It's rather nice.

I head into town and follow Bridge Street to the Castle. Standing under the perpendicular walls of the double-tower gate I wonder at the audacity of the Normans. I can see the grooves the iron portcullis slid down, and the murder holes for dropping boiling oil or molten lead on attackers. From directly below, the Marten tower is huge and the wall daunting. The north wall sits directly on the limestone cliffs that rise from the river. On the town side, the path

Severn Crossing, Sedbury and start of Offa's Dyke

below the castle winds through woodland and I follow it. Above me, below the castle's curtain wall, a group of children wave to me and laugh. This looks an exciting place to play. There is another gatehouse at the west end, different but no less formidable.

The tide is in and a sign next to the old bridge says that the river has the highest tidal range in the world at 14m. The bridge, I read, was built by John Urpeth Rastrick, who chaired the panel judging the Rainhill trials of Stevenson's Rocket in 1829.

The Wye Valley, around Chepstow, was one of the first areas in England to be industrialized. There was plenty of water, wood and coal and flat-bottomed sailing ships called "trows" sailed from Hereford via Chepstow, to Bristol. Men called "bow hauliers" were hired to pull the trows through the shallow water. Paper mills, shipyards, wire-making factories and foundries were set up along the river and oak bark was traded for Irish tanneries. With the opening of the Wye Valley Railway in 1876, trading on the river ended. Today the railroad no longer exists, and nature has reclaimed the abandoned industrial sites.

The Panevino restaurant didn't have my booking, but they found a table for me in the window. The tomato and basil soup is thick and delicious, the ciabatta bread dripping in olive oil and the green pesto dip superb.

Chepstow Castle gatehouse

Old Wye Bridge

The Romans built a crossing a kilometre upstream of the current bridge at Chepstow and the Normans built a wooden bridge across the river close to its current site. Over the centuries, this wooden bridge was replaced several times, Gloucester, and less prosperous Monmouthshire, being responsible for their respective halves.

Built in 1816, the current bridge was designed by John Rastrick as five elegant cast iron arches resting on tapering piers of squared ashlar. The bridge is the largest iron arch road bridge remaining from before the innovation of suspension bridges. Carrying the main road between Gloucester and South Wales, the bridge became a notorious bottleneck and was strengthened several times. It now carries local traffic.

I wander by the river after dinner. There are limestone caves high above the water line. Later I search on-line but find no evidence of them being occupied. But just a mile downstream, on my side of the river, St Peter's Cave

Chepstow Bridge - largest tidal range in world

was occupied by Stone-Age man and wooly mammoth bones have been found there.

The more famous King Arthur's Cave is also next to the River Wye, near where I'm going tomorrow, 3 miles to the north-east of Monmouth. The cave sits about 300 feet above the river and has a broad entrance platform, a double interconnected entrance and two main chambers, one about 25 feet in diameter. It was occupied during the Upper Palaeolithic 20,000 years ago. Flint tools and the bones of woolly mammoth, lion, brown bear, rhinoceros, elk and reindeer bones have been unearthed there. There is a local legend that Vortigern, a British king who fought the Anglo-Saxons, died nearby.

River Wye, high tide below caves

Day 2 Chepstow to Tintern

Monday 13th of June (9 miles)

The tide is high as I cross the old bridge and climb the steep alleyway to join the Offa's Dyke path. It's a fine sunny day, warm in the sun with a light breeze. The path winds through meadows, past large houses in extensive grounds. Some serious money here. There is a beautiful arts and crafts mansion with elegant tall brick chimneys and an ostentatious folly with green turrets and a great view over horse paddocks towards Chepstow. Then a modern affair with a ridiculous garden dotted randomly with classical sculptures and clipped topiary in the form of inverted cones.

I was seduced down a lane by a footpath sign and a woman popped out of her cottage and put me right. 'Not all footpaths are the Offa's Dyke', she admonished me. 'Look out for the acorns!!'. At Wintour's Leap the narrow path follows the cliff edge with only a wire fence between you and a long drop. There is a huge, abandoned quarry next to the river and I imagine them getting

Looking back to Chepstow Castle

the stone for the castle from here and transporting it down river by barge.

No wonder there were settlements along here as far as Gloucester and Shrewsbury. The river is still tidal this far inland, and this must have been the easiest way to get around. Robin and Black Caps are singing their hearts out and there is a pervasive smell of garlic, not unpleasant. I can see Tintern Abbey through the trees and the path descends out of the woods and across fields to Brockweir and the bridge.

I call Jays Taxi. I had booked him for 4pm and it's now only 11am. 'So early', he says, and agrees to meet me at Tintern Abbey in an hour. I could have got to Monmouth in one day. Nevermind, I'm easing myself in. There is a grassy path by the river and then a short climb up to the old railway station. There are tables and people. It's most pleasant and I stop for coffee and home-made lemonade.

It's a trek along the road through Tintern. A bus goes past, and I check the times at the bus stop and realise I could have got a bus instead of a taxi. Too late. The Abbey is as impressive as the castle – just as tall and near the river. My driver announces he's a railway enthusiast and regales me with facts and dates about various lines including the Chepstow to Monmouth line, now defunct.

Wintour's Leap

Tintern Abbey, William Wordsworth, July 13, 1798

Five years have past; five summers, with the length
Of five long winters! and again I hear
These waters, rolling from their mountain-springs
With a soft inland murmur. - Once again
Do I behold these steep and lofty cliffs,
That on a wild secluded scene impress
Thoughts of more deep seclusion; and connect
The landscape with the quiet of the sky. ...

That after many wanderings, many years
Of absence, these steep woods and lofty cliffs,
And this green pastoral landscape, were to me
More dear, both for themselves and for thy sake!

The Old Station, Tintern

Tintern Abbey

Tintern Abbey was founded in 1131 on the Welsh bank of the River Wye and was the first Cistercian foundation in Wales, and only the second in Britain. It was mostly rebuilt during the 13th century, and it is this Gothic abbey church that can be seen today. It is built of Old Red Sandstone with a cruciform plan. The abbey fell into ruin after the Dissolution of the Monasteries in the 16th century. Valuables from the Abbey were sent to the royal Treasury and Abbot Wych was pensioned off. Lead from the roof was sold and the decay of the buildings began.

I've been feeling my aches and pains today and weighing up how I'm doing. My toes ache with arthritis and my hip hurts. But my knee, which was what I was worried about, feels okay. But it's been a short day and there are much longer to come.

I have been daydreaming about the Normans and what a shock they must have been to the Anglo-Saxons in their small hamlets. I imagine trying to take

Tintern Abbey

> **Chepstow Castle**
>
> Chepstow Castle is the oldest surviving post-Roman stone fortification in Britain and the southernmost of a chain of castles built in the Welsh Marches. Construction began in 1067, only a year after the Conquest, on a narrow limestone ridge between the river cliff and the Dell. The site overlooked an important crossing of the River Wye. The castle has four baileys, added in turn through its history. Despite not a being a defensively strong castle, it was nevertheless occupied by the most powerful medieval magnates, including William Marshall and Richard de Clare. By the 1700s it had fallen into decay. It is now a popular visitor destination.

the castle. The gate might have been the weak point.

After a rest, I sally forth to buy a toothbrush and get back just too late to go round the castle. Nevertheless, the Guardian let me in to the lower Bailey. The Great Tower was completed by 1090 from Stone quarried locally. The twin tower gatehouse was added by William Marshall in the 1190s, a hundred years later.

Chepstow Casle

Day 3 Brockweir Bridge to Monmouth

Tuesday 14 June (9 miles)

Breakfast, then a taxi to Brockweir Bridge. I'm going well this morning. Blue sky, puffy clouds, heavy dew on the young summer grass. The river is full and there is a line of flotsam and jetsam that almost keeps pace with me as the tide flows inland. Birdsong and green abundance. Sheep with lambs in a water meadow. I stop for a comfort break on a tree that forms a handy seat.

The tide flows on. Remarkable, so much I don't know. How did the economy of this land work when the Cistercians let land to tenants? How does it work now? I can't believe people are living from the land anymore. And how did people navigate this river, what produce did they transport, how did it all work? There are houses scattered through the woods on the other side of the river, but few will work on the land anymore.

I have a yen to boat down the river from its source to the sea. I am watching the debris in the stream wondering when it will halt. It seems to slow. Then a

Brockweir Bridge

minute later and it is flowing strongly downstream in the opposite direction. Slack water is barely a minute long.

Four Cormorant fly past, two land and then take off again in a flurry of wing beats and splashing. The water meadow is lush but with only a few species of grasses, meadow buttercup and a patch of sorrel. Another Mallard and five big chicks. A fallen tree in the river and two swans hidden in the foliage. Delicate blue damselflies dancing in unison on the path by ripening corn. A beautiful grand house, possibly the owner of all this land, river, and hillside.

I come upon three fishermen brewing up on the tailgate of their SUV as they wait for the river to fall. 'We were fishing but we were up to our waists on the jetty and had to get out', says one of them. 'What do you fish?' 'Salmon and Chard and Bass', one of them says. 'We don't catch much, but it's being in nature that's the thing. How far are you walking?' 'Only to Monmouth.' 'Only! That's 8 miles.' 'How far does the tide come up'; I ask? 'On up to Wyeseal Farm, about half a mile upriver.'

The river has turned from muddy brown to slate grey that reflects the cow parsley growing on the opposite bank. Bigweir Bridge, then a stretch of road. Birdsong as I enter Highbury Wood – Jay and Wood Warbler, Wren, Tree Creeper and Blackbird. And the trees – English Oak and Willow Oak, Beech

River Wye, just above tidal range

Highbury Wood

Cadora and Highbury Woods are ancient. Highbury Wood is an example of ancient semi-natural woodland typical of the Wye Valley until the 1950s. It was managed for centuries by coppicing to provide wood for charcoal and fuel for the lime kilns. Coppice management has been revived to create a woodland structure that favours a wide range of wildlife including, dormice, butterflies, and many different woodland flowers. Lime and Whitebeam, as well as Oak, are more than 300 years old. Nuhatches, Tree Creepers and Woodpeckers are amongst the birds that nest in the woodland.

and 300-year-old Yew. These woods are ancient, untidy, and complex. Something russet flashes past – a fox, or maybe just a squirrel with the sun on its tail.

Now I'm skirting the wood through sloping parkland. A Painted Lady butterfly dancing along in front of me, alighting momentarily in time with my footfall. A young man passes me with a solar panel tied to his rucksack, like the one I used on the Pennine Way. He says he's going from Lands' End to John O'Groats, wild

Highbury Wood - ancient coppiced trees

camping. I'm impressed. Later, in Redbrook, I catch him up as he enters a village store. I follow and get a coffee from the machine, and we sit outside chatting convivially. We talk about walking. He's doing Offa's Dyke until he reaches the canal at Chirk and will then follow it towards the Peak and onto Edale. He then walks the Pennine Way as far as Hadrian's Wall. 'That's most of it', he says. 'Hardly', I say. 'The best is yet to come in the Tees, Tyne, and Cheviots.' 'I could go that way, but I have a friend in Glasgow, he says.' 'And then the Highland Way?' 'Yes, he says.' 'How long will it take?' 'I planned on three months, but I think it will only be 2 1/2. I haven't done anything like this before and hadn't ever wild camped. It's good, but the isolation gets to you.'

I tell him about my Pennine Way trip during lockdown. 'You end up talking to yourself, singing some daft tune, and counting steps.' 'Yes, I whistle badly', he says, 'and sing. But you cover the ground. After Glastonbury I climbed a hill and looked back and could see my route for miles. Long days. Some 20+ and one 28 miles'. 'Yes. Even me, at my slow pace, walking all day, you do the mileage.'

We introduce ourselves. His name is George. He practised on the Southwest Coast Path and tried out the gear and camping. We talk about food – dried food, couscous, and tuna. 'It gets bland', he says. 'How did you get on the Pennine Way?' I tell him I carried everything in six-day stretches with two post-

George, walking Land's End to John O'Groats

restante drops. He's staying with friends and relatives on the way when he can. 'You have to take advantage of a bath now and then', he says. In the Wye Valley he camped overlooking Tintern and bathed in the river. It must have been mucky I thought. 'It was nice', he said.

There is a long pull up from Redbrook along the road, and George leaves me far behind. Then a stony lane and finally a path through woods. It is hot and hard, and I stop for an apple at Kymin National Trust car park. There is a monument, a Naval Temple, dedicated to "those Noble Admirals who distinguished themselves by their glorious victories".

From here it's all downhill into Monmouth. I cross the bridge over the Wye and make my way to the centre. A pedestrian street leads to Agincourt Square. Henry V was born here, and his statue is on the front of the town hall. And there's my digs for the night – the Punch House – a pub with outside tables in the square.

I've unpacked and washed my clothes and am sitting in the sunshine listening to Test Match Special, first at a cafe with tea and chocolate cake, and then on a bench on the High Street. It's the fifth day of the second test at Headingley, and Bairstow and Stokes are winning a famous victory for England, no less astonishing than Agincourt, and I feel part of it, although I'm only participating

Navel Temple, Kymin

> **Naval temple**
>
> The Naval Temple was constructed by the Kymin Club in 1800 to commemorate the second anniversary of the Battle of the Nile in 1798 and to acknowledge the victories of sixteen of the British Royal Navy's Admirals. The monument is a flamboyant, colourful classical structure with two porticos and Doric columns. The Monmouth Picnic Club of local gentry, the Kymin Club, met weekly in the nearby Round House to dine and socialise. Nelson visited Monmouth and the Temple in 1802, along with Lady Hamilton and her husband, Sir William Hamilton.

through listening to the radio on my phone.

I have a delicious fish and chips and mushy pea supper eaten in Aslan's fish and chip shop round the corner. Then an early night with the test match highlights on BBC Two again on my phone. And, surprisingly, since the sixes and fours are so sensational, it's not as exciting as hearing it relayed through the voices of the TMS commentators.

Agincourt Square and statue of Henry V, Monmouth

Monmouth, Trefynwy (10,500)

Monmouth is situated where the River Monnow joins the River Wye. The town was the site of a small Roman fort, Blestium, and became established after the Normans built Monmouth Castle c.1067. A town grew up around the castle, and a Benedictine priory was established in 1075. Geoffrey of Monmouth, writer of Historia Regum Britanniae (History of the Kings of Britain) was born here around 1100. The town walls were built in c.1300, and the bridge over the Monnow was fortified. The medieval stone gated bridge is the only one of its type remaining in Britain. King Henry V was born in the castle in 1386.

Fish and chip supper at Aslan's

Day 4 Monmouth to Pandy

Wednesday 15 June (16 miles)

I get away soon after 7am after breakfasting in my room on croissant and yoghurt, courtesy of M&S. It's another fine day. Blue sky and the merest of breezes. I walk down the High Street. Monmouth seems prosperous and vibrant with its many independent shops. A mother and toddler catch me up. He's about three and has a little knapsack, with his lunch I suppose. He breaks into a stumbling run, then stops to admire the road sweeper that woke me at 6am. The driver honks his horn as he drives past. The little boy is delighted, then crestfallen as he sees it disappearing in the distance. He runs to try and catch it. 'He never runs like this to school, his mother says. He looks back at me, crosses his feet and tumbles headfirst. 'Oh dear', I say, as he looks at me with accusing eyes.

There is a tower gate on the bridge over the Monnow, a stream that gives the town its name. Then along Watery Lane. a driver gingerly crosses a

Tower Gate over River Monnow, Monmouth

concrete bridge over the canalised brook that runs between the houses and the carriageway. An old man jogs past me and slows to chat. 'Are you under canvas?' 'No, I'm B&Bing'. 'Quite right, a comfortable bed for the night. I'll carry on jog-walking', he says, and sets off again.

I leave the habitation and skirt a field of wheat before entering Hendre Wood and climb to the ridge. It's cool and pleasant in the shade. Then a descent to Hendre. The two or three farms all do camping and B&B. They look prosperous. A tractor driver is turning the hay. Fat sheep with fat lambs, and a herd of white Charolais cattle standing quietly under the trees. It's getting hot now and I stop on a bench a kindly farmer has placed next to the path. The fields are bounded by good hedges and venerable oaks. The farms have changed to the modern way of intensive farming with huge barns. The meadows and fields uniform, but this is not a denuded landscape. There are trees, hedges, and woodland and plenty of birdlife. Above me there is a mob of 50 or 60 crows circling in the thermals. The land looks productive, but there is still room for some nature. A delicate bright Yellow Hammer flutters in the tree above where I'm sitting.

Hay meadows by Afron Trothy. Someone has walked straight across, but I'm constrained to follow the field's edge as it follows the winding stream. Fields of Meadow Buttercup and Clover. Fat lambs. A water tap by a horse paddock

Farmer turning hay

where I fill my water bottle and take a long cool swig. Different breeds of cattle – brown and white and black and white Hereford and deep chocolate Redpoll.

I cross a cider apple orchard, the trees in straight rows. I meet a woman doing the walk in bits north to south. 'Nice and flat today, but too hot', she says. 'Are you going all the way? It's a climb for you tomorrow then the long 10-mile ridge. I did it in two stretches'.

There is a sign on the gate at Tre-Adam suggesting you ring to see if the pub, the Hogshead, is open. It is, and I order a pint of orange and tonic. The landlord is dramatically overweight, has a brace on his leg and rides a mobility scooter. His face is red and blotchy, and he looks most unwell. Poor guy. He's pleasant and friendly and tells me they had 60 caravans last weekend and are expecting 300 to 400 guests this coming weekend. There is a security camera in the bar. Perhaps it can get quite rowdy. A field of green wheat that I give it the "Gladiator' stroke.

From here to White Castle, you descend through sheep meadows. The castle is impressive, with its moat and gatehouse. I'm tired and I'm a bit on autopilot for the next stretch to Llangattock. Two buzzards fly over my head and land in trees.

White Castle gatehouse

> **White Castle**
>
> White Castle faced hill country controlled by Welsh lords and was the first to have its wooden structure replaced with stone. Conflict in the 13th Century required a garrison of several thousand and the castle has a sophisticated gatehouse and a large inner and outer ward. In the event of the attack never came and White Castle never saw action.

In Llangattock there is an ancient church dedicated to the Celtic St. Cadoc and, near the altar, a wooden bier on which corpses were carried and buried in shrouds rather than coffins. The bier is a body-shaped plank suspended in a frame on short legs with handles. I reach the nearby Hunters Moon Inn and have another pint of orange and tonic. The sun has come out again and it's warm and tough doing the last couple of miles across the fields to Pandy. I reach the main road where the path goes left and have another mile along the road to the Old Pandy Inn in the opposite direction. It's hard walking along a hard main road at the end of the day if it's in the wrong direction. I try hitching without success and buckle down to walk it.

St Cadoc Church, Llangattock

> **Death in Llangattock**
>
> Llan in a place name denotes a sacred burial site. From early mediaeval times burials were either inside the church, for important people, or in shallow graves on the south side of the churchyard. The bier in St Cadoc's Church, dated 1711, is a rare survival of a burial practice where the body was wrapped in a shroud without a coffin. The body was placed on the bier and a wooden framework, called the hearse, was placed over the body and a black cloth, the pall was draped over. The party carrying the deceased from home to the church gate was led by the Sexton and Parson. The bier, hearse and pall were then stored ready for the next burial.

I try to check-in and the landlady seems nonplussed when I say I'm booked in for the night, and she shows me to a bunk room. I wash my clothes, shower, and ring Scharlie. Then I get a call from woman in Abergavenny who asks me where I am. It seems I'm booked with her. She said she would come and collect me and take me to a pub for a meal tonight. 'I've got everything ready', she says. I feel awful and am about to suggest that I pack my stuff and then I think better of it and just apologise profusely. I half remember talking to her and making the booking. I'm intrigued to know what language the landlord and landlady are speaking. I ask if it is Romanian, and she says yes. I order a meal of sausage and mash and get an early night.

> **Pandy (1900)**
>
> A hamlet without a parish church at the foot of the Black Mountains. Pandy means fulling in Welsh (to wash sheep's wool) and there was a mill here the 17th Century. Raymond Williams, socialist philosopher, and novelist was born in Pandy in a cottage next to Offa's Dyke where his father was a railway signalman on the Hereford to Abergavenny railway line.

The 'bier' in Llangattock church

Day 5 Pandy to Hay-on-Wye

Thursday 16 June (16 miles)

I woke before the alarm at 6am and was at breakfast by 7am – Coco Pops and coffee. I could have had a cooked breakfast but skipped it to get away early. The way was straightforward, through an iron lynch gate and the estate of Tre-Wyn House.

The lane climbs, contouring the slope, until the Offa's Dyke Path is gained. Then it's a climb up the grassy ridge and a delightfully long ridge walk. Blue skies, skylarks, and wild ponies. I bash on and stop at a trig point about halfway to put on my knee support. I'm doing okay, body holding up – just the usual aches and pains – nothing special.

Lych-gate into the Tre-Wyn estate

Small herds of ponies, descendants of pit ponies from Welsh coalfields and the wild horses Raymond Williams suggests Stone Age people's hunted on these same bare ridges. Stallions with 4 to 9 mares, black, dun, white and grey; I imagine they command territories jealously.

I read Raymond Williams' first book "The Beginnings", about the people of the Black Mountain's, over 30 years ago. Using the barest of clues from the archaeological record, the book recreates the imagined lives of people in the Wye Valley and the Black Mountains, from a stone-age family 25,000 years ago, till the arrival of the Romans in 51AD. I re-read it when I got back home, and his second book, "The Eggs of the Eagle", that takes the story on till the Battle of Agincourt in 1415. Sadly, Raymond died before he was able to complete the trilogy and bring the story up to the present day.

What his writing does is bring history alive. It paints a complex pattern of change, of strife and community, of a relentless quest for survival and advancement and how man has adapted to and transformed the land. It puts my feeble attempts to understand the shape and character of the places along the Dyke into perspective. Since the ice, over thousands of years, different peoples, with the same hopes and fears as us, have lived and worked in the Black Mountains.

Trig point on ridge above Hatterall Hill

The Black Mountains

The Black Mountains (Y Mynydd Duon) are a group of hills in southeast Wales, extending across the England–Wales border into Herefordshire, and are the easternmost of the ranges that comprise the Brecon Beacons National Park. In People of the Black Mountains, Raymond Williams described the Black Mountains thus: "See this layered sandstone in the short mountain grass. Place your right hand on it, palm downward. See where the summer sun rises and where it stands at noon. Direct your index finger midway between them. Spread your fingers, not widely. You now hold this place in your hand."

The Black Mountains are composed almost exclusively of Old Red Sandstone dating from the Devonian period. The area lay at the margins of the British icesheet and these hills were shaped by ice. The range includes the highest public road in Wales, at Gospel Pass, and the highest point in southern England, at Black Mountain.

Herd of ponies - a stallion with half a dozen or so mares

It makes me think about how bedrock geology determines how the land resisted the grinding force of glaciers, what can grow on the land and what minerals lie beneath its surface and have been exploited by man. The legacy of the ice can be seen in uplands and watercourses, in erratics and moraine. And I think about the impact of man – quarrying and mining, hunting and grazing, clearing forest, damming, and diverting rivers, and building homes, bridges, temples, and workshops. It's so overwhelming it makes my head spin. By extension the whole of Britain is like this, yet we can't see it clearly or take heed of what it means for our future.

The ridge goes on, benign and safe today in the clear sunlight; less so, I imagine, in a winter storm. Heather, sedge and cotton grass and close-cropped sward; the path worn with many feet, with new growth fostered by the ponies' dry manure. It's pleasant on the grass, less so on the stone path that crosses the sandstones boggy bits. They're dry today after the long spell of dry weather we've had. The geology is like the Peak, with peat overlying gritstone. There are occasional black pools, so the ponies have water. I half wish I had a water-filter like George told me he carried, so I could sample the cool Coca-Cola coloured liquid. I remember the black water of the Upper Orinoco where all you had to do was to dip a mug over the side of the dugout chalana to get a drink.

Hay Bluff, Pen y Begwn

I'm accompanied by the sound of skylarks. I've left Chris and Pearl far behind. I met them yesterday and we walked together for a while. They have done many of the long walks, including the Pennine Way and West Highland Way. 'We tried the Pennine Way for the second time last year and got as far as Horton in Ribblesdale in atrocious weather and had to give up', they say. They ask me what I've done, and I mention the GR20 in Corsica.

I've reached Hay Bluff, Pen y Begwn, and have stopped on a grassy bank where there is a breeze. I have two nut bars for lunch and drink lots of water. I've taken my boots and socks off and lathered my sore toes in Compeed gel. I'll get going in a minute, but it's nice here in the breeze.

It's hard starting off. My hip hurts and I'm feeling doddery going downhill. Going down is worse than going up, although both are hard in different ways. Going down is hard on the knees and thighs; I can't skip down like I used to. And going up is hard for obvious reasons. The trick is to just plod on. If you're feeling good, you can think about controlling your breathing and place your feet carefully and precisely. If you're struggling, you just have to shut off, banish care, and keep going, trying not to look up too often to see how far it is to the top of the next rise, and not being too disappointed when the supposed top is just a dip in the slope and there's more to do.

Orchids in meadow grass

There are hundreds of maroon ground orchids in a meadow of yellow buttercups. I'm close, but the last two miles always seem a long way. Finally, I'm down. The young man, who has been following me, catches me up. He's German, and this is his first-time walking in the UK. I usually walk in the Alps, he says. We introduce ourselves. Franz lives in Munich. I tell him that we're going to a wedding in Germany in July in Karlsruhe. 'It used to be nice', he says. We talk about Brexit. 'It won't affect us as much as it will you', he says. 'I have English friends, educated; they voted to leave. Taking back control - from what? Everything is connected in this global world', he says.

I find the Swan Inn. No one about and it's like the Marie Celeste. I go investigating. A young man appears and gets his manager, another young man. I ask for a quiet room and get one round the side, where I can still hear the road. I go down and order a pint of orange and tonic and sit in the garden and watch a tame Blackbird hopping about. Doing nothing, stopping still – it's nice. Back in my room with a ginger beer, I check what time they serve breakfast – not till 8am. Pity, since I want to make an early start because tomorrow will be hot. I watch an hour of women's football – England v. Belgium. I've got to know the players and they're good. It was 2-0 to England when I called it a day and tried to sleep.

Garden of the Swan Inn, Hay-on-Wye

Hay-on-Wye, Y Gelli (1600)

Market town renowned for books and bookshops. Hay has two Norman castles – a motte and bailey castle at the western edge of the town and a stone castle on a commanding site in the centre. Since 1988 the town has held an annual book festival in June that draws 80,000 visitors. The town still has two dozen bookshops. Bill Clinton described Hay as "The Woodstock of the mind".

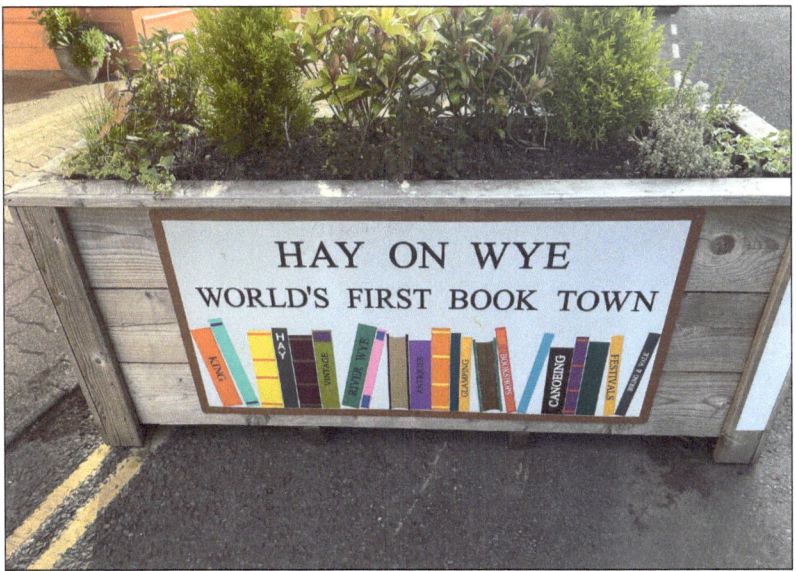

Hay-on-Wye, Y Gelli

Day 6 Hay-on-Wye to Kingston

Friday 17 June (15 miles)

As forecast, it dawned bright and promised a scorcher. I woke before 6am and packed, and rather than wait till 8am I went down and found some of the breakfast stuff out and was able to down muesli, fresh fruit salad and two glasses of orange. I need to keep hydrated today.

A getaway at 7.30. I'm pleased. I walk down the pedestrianised shopping street rather than the main road and come to the castle. As advertised, there are lots of bookshops. There is a bridge over the Wye. The river is wide here and someone is fishing upstream where the water looks black and still.

The path follows the river north along grassy water meadows. It's already getting warm. Santa and Romain, the French couple I saw sleeping in the grassy moat of White Castle, pass me while I'm peeing in the bushes. We exchange pleasantries at a gate and leapfrog each other. There is steep section of road and then you enter the cool shady woods of Bettws Dingle. It's the majestic old

Bookshops on Castle Street, Hay-on-Wye

Hay Castle

Deeply rutted track through an avenue of trees

oaks that give the best shade and it feels distinctly cooler under their spreading branches. Another stretch of road. They are haymaking in the adjacent fields. Most farmers have already baled their hay. The track is deeply rutted but attractive, since it's an avenue of trees – hazel, hawthorn, beech, birch, and rowan. Two buzzards circling overhead. They look big enough to be eagles.

I've been weighing up the farming practices on the Dyke. Some fields have been left fallow, but most are intensively grazed with sheep and cattle. I come to a couple of bare fields ready for planting a winter crop and see that the soil looks dead. They'll need artificial fertiliser. A meadow has been spread with muck rather than slurry. A large pile of bailed hay in black plastic – shards of plastic scattered all around where bails have been unwrapped

I get to Newchurch and catch up with Pearl and Chris. They tell me I can make coffee or tea inside the church. Santa and Romain arrive, and we chat. Like Chris and Pearl, they're camping. They say Chris told them I'd done the GR20 across Corsica. Santa says she is Corsican and would like to do it but thought it might be too challenging. They did the Pennine Way as far as Horton last year and want to go back and complete it. They met as medical students in Paris. 'But we won't don't want to live in big cities any longer', says Santa. 'We're going to move to a village near Toulouse', says Romain. I make tea. We

Romain making tea in Newchurch

leave some change in the donation box. It's nice and trusting that they leave the churches open.

From here you climb a steep grassy path up Disgwylfa Hill. It's easy walking but it's hot and my feet hurt, and I plod on. The ridge flattens out and it's pleasant, contouring with the hill along the wide grass track. The track descends a gully to reach the village of Gladestry and I find the pub, The Oak, and order my usual drink and a plate of pitta bread and houmous. The young barmaid wants to chat, until a couple arrive and I'm able to return to my journal.

There is a long climb up the lane, tarmac at first. Finally, I reach the soft grass track. The cough has settled on my chest, and I feel lightheaded and a bit dizzy with the heat and the sun feels murderous. The rest I gave my feet at the Oak pub has helped and the turf is soft, as promised by the barmaid. What an appropriate name – it's the oaks that have been my salvation today. The two buzzards are following me. There are skylarks and pipits. It would be delightful if it wasn't so hot, and I didn't feel so unwell. Santa and Romain catch me up while I'm sitting on a rock drinking my remaining water. It's nice chatting and it helps take one's mind off the aches and pains and how far I still have to go.

We get to the Burton Hotel, my digs for the night. It's old-fashioned and

The Oak, Gladestry

elegant and I buy Romain and Santa drinks. I get a Covid test kit and discover that, I'm positive. What a shock, I figure it was the crowded train or the taxi I took from Tintern back to Chepstow on Monday afternoon. No wonder I've been struggling and feeling under-the-weather. This new variant must be very contagious. Three years without getting it! I was just thinking how clever I've been. I had a fever in the night. How ironic to get Covid now, when I thought it was all over and I'd need a different title for my journal.

Kington (2600)

The Anglo-Saxon settlement on the site was devastated by the Normans and became part of a Marcher barony. Kington passed to the Crown after the incumbent baron rebelled in 1174. Situated on the drover route from Hergest Ridge and with eight annual fairs, Kington grew in importance as a market town, and there is still a thriving livestock market on Thursdays. The town retains its medieval grid pattern of streets and back lanes.

Grassy track up Hergest Ridge to Kington

Day 7 Kington to Knighton

Saturday 18 June (13 miles)

It dawns grey, and mercifully cooler. Last night swifts were buzzing round the tower just in front of my window. I'm feeling rough – not surprising really. The waitress looks Filipino – so many foreigners keeping our tourism going. She is attentive and good at her job. It's drizzling as I leave, and I stop under the glass canopy in front of the hotel to put on my anorak. I think I must have taken the wrong road out of town and stop to ask a dog-walker and he says, I don't suppose you want to go back, and directs me down a lane to a bridge across the brook.

It's hard to remember the day. I was struggling until I took a couple of paracetamol, which seemed to give me a boost. It's marvellous that the Dyke is so prominent. In fact, for much of the way you walk along the top of the Dyke. It's not that high. Maybe up to 2m in places but because it's an earth mound with sloping sides, it is less impressive than the vertical Hadrian's Wall.

View from my room in Burton Hotel

Nevertheless, it must have been a huge undertaking.

Leaving Kington there is a twisted trunk embedded in the wall. Interestingly although one sees the occasional dead elm like a portent of the Apocalypse, the ash are still looking healthy. This is amazingly fertile land. There are fields of peas that have been left to fix nitrogen. A huge Red Kite sailing over the moors on the edge of the farmland. Yellow Rattle in the meadows, and, like yesterday, there is Mares Tail along the path where it's been carried on people's boots. (Mare's Tail is the last remnant of the Equisetaceae family of plants that thrived during the Devonian period, hundreds of millions of years ago.)

Climbing to the moor, a couple of shepherds are docking sheep's tails and worming. The older man – wizened with bronze cheeks and snow-white hair smiles and says, 'Not the day for it, but has to be done'. The younger man, his son I assume, is bent over a sheep, and doesn't look up, cutting off the dags on one of the sheep's tails.

Foxgloves in the hedgerows. It drizzles all day, but the forecast downpour doesn't happen. Rolling hills, lush green valleys. But the long grass soaks one's boots and Romain and Santa, who I meet at a stile, complain that their feet are wet. That will be a problem for them camping.

I'm in the spectacular community centre in Knighton, in the huge hall. I've

Twisted trunk in wall in Kington

come over to see if I can get a cup of tea and a place to sit while I wait for the bus to Knucklas, where I'm booked in at the Castle Inn. I've landed on my feet; the County Show, organised by the local Women's Institute, is in full swing and I get a cheese sandwich, a scone topped with cream and a strawberry and a cup of tea.

Google says my bus is about to arrive, so I leave the community centre and walk over to the bus shelter. The shelter has seen better days and, with its perforated panels, offers little shelter from wind or rain.

The landlady at the Castle Inn is Thai and takes no prisoners. She seems very competent, and the menu is huge, varied and has vegetarian options. The restaurant is full of locals eating out – it's Saturday night.

The Dyke in the mist north of Kington

Knighton, Tref-y-clawdd (3000)

Knighton is another border town. The Welsh name, Tref-y-clawdd, means "town on the dyke". It became a borough in 1203, with a charter permitting a weekly market and annual fair. Knighton first prospered as a centre of the wool trade in the 15th century and was later an important point on two drover routes. Bryn y Castell was besieged by Owain Glyndŵr in 1402 and destroyed along with much of the town. Knighton is now on the railway line from Craven Arms to the Mumbles.

Knucklas, Cnwclas (220)

Knucklas is 3 miles north-west of Knighton and lies in the upper valley of the River Teme. Knucklas railway station is on the Heart of Wales Line. The castle consisted of a square stone keep with four round towers. It was captured and destroyed by a Welsh army in 1262 and only the mound remains. The site is linked to the marriage of Guinevere and King Arthur. The spectacular 13-arch span was completed by the Central Wales Railway in 1865. Three Bronze Age torcs were found nearby.

Fine old barn, Evenjobb, Presteigne, Powys

Day 8 Knucklas to Montgomery

Sunday 19 June (19 miles)

It's dry today and cool. Being Sunday in Wales, there are no buses, so I head up to the Dyke from here rather than trying to get back to Knighton. I'll only miss some of what looks from the map to be good day. The landlady, Ying, has agreed to serve breakfast at 7.30 rather than 8am. I have two poached eggs, which seem to do me good because I have more energy today. But it is a long, tough day, not only because of the 19 miles but also because of the three big ascents and steep descents that follow the line of the wall. First, though, I have to reach the Dyke which involves crossing a field to the road, then a climb to the ridge where I join the path from Knighton at Garbett Hall.

The wall is remarkably dominant – distinct and prominent in the landscape and the path follows it to Llanfair Hill. Kites soaring. The dike is heavily treed here and there is a birdsong concert from Song Thrush, Firecrest and Blackbird. No sign of Romain and Santa or Chris and Pearl, who started from Knighton.

Offa's Dyke, near Llanfair Hill

The path descends to Spoad, and an ancient farmhouse painted bright yellow, just along the road from Newcastle, followed by the first of the steep hills up Bryn y Cratch.

These Shropshire Hills are designated as an Area of Outstanding Beauty. I walked Long Mynd many years ago, which is to the east, but hadn't quite appreciated that between Knighton and Montgomery would be the best preserved and most spectacular section of the Dyke. Nor had I appreciated that this would be the most undulating and demanding part of the walk. This is border country or Marches, with Offa's Dyke the visible evidence of the border between England and Wales, and the dividing line between two different cultures.

There is more up-and-down to Churchtown. On the path near Middle Knuck I find a paper on the grass. It looks like someone's itinerary, and I put it in my pocket. Further on I meet two women walking the path, Sally and Jackie, and it's theirs. 'It's a work of art', I say. Like me, they're going to the Dragon Inn in Montgomery. Further on I stop and sit on a stile until they catch me up and I ask them if I can take a photograph of the paper for my journal. 'Are you joking', they say, intrigued? 'Yes, unless you keep a Journal you forget.' 'That's right, it was like that on the Dales Walk and on the Pilgrim's Way', they say.

Yellow farmhouse at Spoad Hill by the River Clun

I set off again up the brutally steep slope that I had seen it from across the valley and had been daunted by. Nevertheless, I plod up it and stop for lunch at the top – take off my boots and socks and rest. Then I put mini Compeed plasters on three small toes that always give trouble. This time I've caught them in good time, before any blisters have had a chance to form.

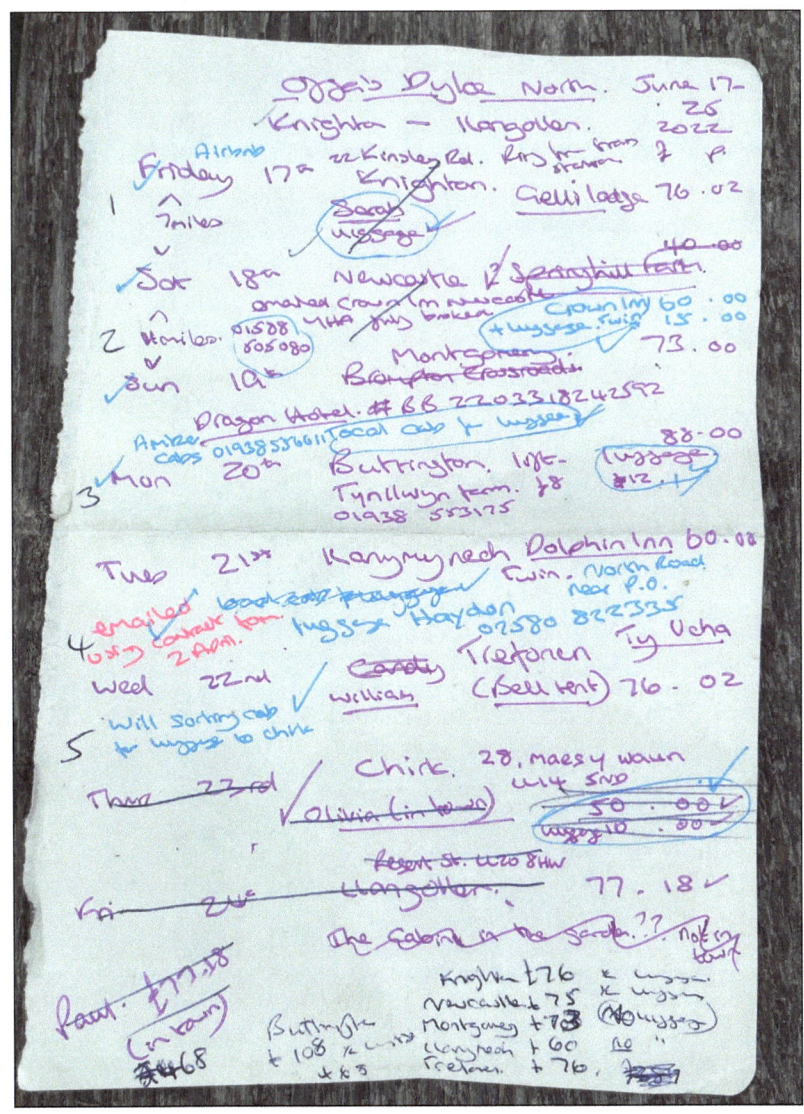

Sally's itinerary for the Northern section of Offa's Dyke walk

A dead mole – big white claws and blind eyes. A huge red kite circling above me. Then later a hawk, maybe a Hen Harrier, with what might have been a baby rook in its beak, being mobbed by corvids.

There are many ancient oaks along the wall, maybe hundreds of years old. I meet a Dutchman coming the other way and we stop to chat. He's called Kris. 'How are you finding it', I ask? 'It's marvellous', he says, 'I love the oaks. They're dying in the Netherlands's from the caterpillars of an invasive moth from the USA'. I look out over the green hills and am relieved to think it hasn't reached Wales yet. 'It makes you doubt climate change', I say, by way of starting a conversation. 'It's all bullshit', he says. 'I don't think it's happening. You, have you seen any evidence of climate change?' 'I've noticed changes in the weather but that doesn't count, and, over my lifetime, I've seen the retreat of glaciers in the Alps and South America. I believe the science'. 'Which scientists', he says. 'It depends on who you listen to.' 'Most scientists', I say. 'We've had to raise the dikes and seawalls in the Netherlands; it's cost billions. We must do it, and if it doesn't work, we can move.' 'Others might not be able to move so easily', I say. And we agree that that this part of Wales is beautiful and that the Dyke is well worth doing, and we go our separate ways.

One of the many Montgomery Oaks that are dying

Motte and Bailey Castle Mound and River Caebitra, Brompton Hall, Montgomery

Broad Street and Montgomery Town Hall

I was thinking how awful, if all the oaks died, and then, on the final stretch into Montgomery, in the most idyllic countryside, one after another, magnificent ancient oaks are dying or already dead. Naked bleach limbs, an affront to nature – distressing, disturbing, alarming. My advice, do Offa's Dyke before all the oaks die. It is an easy last mile into Montgomery. There is bunting in the square from the Jubilee and the Dragon Hotel is most welcoming.

I feel I've been going well today, but it took me longer than expected. It must have been the hills, the steep ups and downs, or maybe not eating enough. I'm off my food and can only manage half my carbonara. I've lost my savour and the food tastes like straw. It's Covid!

> **Montgomery, Trefaldwyn (1300)**
>
> Only a mile from the border, the town was established around a Norman stone castle on a crag on the western edge of the Vale of Montgomery. Roger de Montgomery, originally from Montgomery in the Pays d'Auge in Normandy, was given this part of the Welsh Marches by William. The striking town hall was built in c.1750. Montgomery railway station is currently closed. Julie Christie lived in a farm on the outskirts of the town.

Dragon Hotel, Montgomery

Day 9 Montgomery to Buttington

Monday 20 June (8 miles)

The day dawns bright and clear and swifts are swooping round the redbrick town hall. A big red van outside the Dragon. Too week to climb to the castle, I set off down the road to walk the two miles to the Dyke. It's flat country to Forden. I run into Chris and Pearl and learn that he is a cabinetmaker. Chris also tells me about sea kayaking in Scotland, which I've always wanted to do. He says they taught themselves. He's been out in big waters of Loch Ness and around Mull. He's done the Caledonian Canal three times, the Seven and the Thames. He says, you should try it. 'I'd need someone to go with', I say.

A timber chalet called Holly Lodge that looks architect designed. Buzzards calling, a crow with a vole in its beak, flying low over the stubble. Getting hot, so I stop to put on sunblock and take a drink. There is a long stretch of Roman Road in a sunken ditch next to the wall, then you enter coniferous woodland and follow a level timber-lorry trail, walking on a bed of pine needles.

Sunken lane running along the side of the wall

Beacon Ring Iron Age hill fort

Beacon ring is a hill fort built in the Iron Age, in the period between about 600 BC and A.D. 50 with a single bank and ditch. Later it was used by Cadwallon, King of the Britons, during the battles with the Northumbrian King Edwin in about A.D. 630. And the forces of Henry Tudor, gathered here in 1485 on the eve of the Battle of Bosworth. It formed part of a chain of signals across the country. Before 1953 the ring was covered in meadow but in 1953, to commemorate the coronation of Elizabeth II, trees were planted inside the hill fort. Clwyd-Powys Agricultural Trust began excavation in 2020 on a slight mound in the middle of the site that was rumoured to be a Bronze Age burial mound. So far, the archaeologists have found a trig point and benchmark with the Board of Ordnance 'broad arrow' symbol from the 'Principal Triangulation' in the 19th century.

The path winds round and joins a road before a long straight climb to Beacon Ring, the Iron Age fort. I've been struggling with Covid all day and am amazed to have caught up with Chris and Pearl at the bottom of the hill. It gives

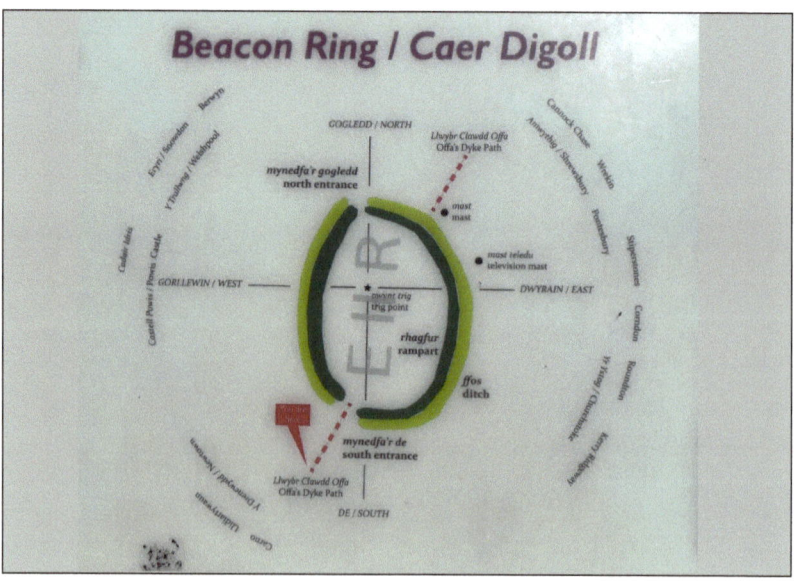

Beacon Ring, Caer Digoll

Track up to Beacon Ring

Royal Oak, Welshpool

me a new lease of life and I plough up at a respectable, steady pace. There is a bench and I stop for lunch – a rather nasty rocky road bar I bought in the Spar in Montgomery because it looked good but is too sugary, with biscuit rather than nut filling.

Pearl arrives just as I am packing up, and, like me, she has to climb the fence, having taken the path on the wrong side of the hedge up the last slope. The ring fort is huge, and a thick dense wood covers the mound. This may be unfortunate, since the site has never been excavated. The path circles the fort until the north entrance and the two big radio masts. From there the grassy path descends through fields, hard on the knees, until the road into Buttington and the Green Dragon.

I stop for a long cool drink and a chicken and bacon baguette, my effort to take in more protein, and repair some of the damage I've been doing to my body. Chris and Pearl arrive and plan to camp here. Maybe I won't see them again as they are planning on doing longer days from now to beat the rail strike.

From Buttington, to Welshpool, a couple of miles away where I'm staying at the Royal Oak, a delightful redbrick coaching inn in the centre town. Once ensconced in my room – all chintz and crystal chandelier, I venture forth to buy more Covid tests at Boots, pumpernickel bread and salami at the Polish

My room in the Royal Oak – all chintz and crystal chandelier,

deli and mackerel and goats' cheese at Morrisons. A long soak in a hot bath, then dinner. Not exactly roughing it, feeling strangely guilty at the contrast with my two previous trips. Thai sweet potato soup and chicken and egg to follow – lots of protein.

> **Welshpool, Y Trallwng (6000)**
>
> A border market town on the River Severn. Initially known only as Pool, the Welsh name translates as marshy or sinking land. The town was devastated by Owain Glyndŵr in 1400 in his rebellion against Henry IV. The octagonal brick building in New Street, was built in the early 18th century and was in continual use as a cockpit until the practice was outlawed by the Cruelty to Animals Act 1849. Welshpool is on the Cambrian railway line. The Montgomery Canal is important for nature and much of it is an SSSI.

Day 10 Welshpool to Llanymynech

Tuesday 21 June (11 miles)

I had a big breakfast at 7am and then a panic attack when I thought I'd lost my sticks and my phone. My sticks were behind the curtains and my phone was in my rucksack. Rather than walk back to Buttington along the busy road or wait for the 9.30 bus, the waiter, an old-boy cyclist, suggests I take the Montgomery Canal towpath.

The canal is beautifully tranquil with waterlilies, swans with cygnets, Canada Geese with goslings and protective moorhens with chicks. You leave the canal and, after a short stretch of road, gain the Dyke and walk along it through water meadows by the side of the River Severn. In a shady glade by the river, two wood chairs and a table with a sign saying cakes. I choose a piece of moist data and walnut and pop a pound coin in the honesty box. A heron takes off as I try to photograph it. Chamomile in tractor and black damselflies dancing above the ripening wheat.

Montgomery Canal and towpath

Montgomery Canal

The Montgomery Canal is one of the most important canals in the country for nature, wildlife thrives along it, much of it is a Site of Special Scientific Interest and the Welsh section is of international importance. Known colloquially as "The Monty" the canal is only partially restored. It ran from from Llanymynech to Newtown but fell out of use in 1936 and was abandoned in 1944.

At present only 7 miles (11 km) is navigable and connected to the rest of the national Canal & River Trust network via the the Ellesmere Canal. Separately, a short stretch at Llanymynech and a central section around Welshpool are also navigable though isolated from the national canal network. Ongoing restoration work continues.

An avenue of ancient oaks on the top of the dike and then you regain the canal. I'm going well and have brief chats with various people about the canal. In the last mile or so there are fallen trees blocking the canal and the locks look in need of major repair.

Delightful glade with cake and honesty box

There is a long aqueduct over the river, a huge engineering feat. All to carry stone from the quarries above Llanymyneck.

I can't believe how narrow the canals are. How did it work when there were lots of barges? Did they have a one-way system? This last stretch of the canal has fallen out of use. The Cross Keys Inn is closed, so I go to the nearby Bradford Arms for lunch.

The jolly landlady at the Cross Keys in Llanymynech is busy serving drinks to building workers who have just finished work. She shows me the room. It's a throwback to the 60s, clean but spartan, which is reflected in the price. I meet Romain on the stairs. He says they're staying here too because there's no campsite. I have dinner at the Dolphin across the road and run into Sally and Jackie, whose paper itinerary I found. They're cousins from Otley in Wharfedale. We talk about the walks were done. They found the Knighton stretch hard. Sally says that on the steep bits she found it difficult to maintain her balance, tipping forwards or backwards.

Locks and stretches of the canal in need of TLC

Llanymynech (1700)

The name is Welsh for "Church of the Monks". The village is on the banks of the River Vyrnwy, and the Montgomery Canal passes through. Llanymynech Hill is one of Wales' earliest mining sites. Copper was mined and smelted here in the late Bronze Age and the hill is crowned with an extensive Iron Age hillfort and surrounds a cave opening known as the Ogof. The Romans extended the cavern and there was mining for silver, lead and copper in the 12th and 13th centuries. Llanymynech is on the Ellesmere / Montgomery Canal, but the stretch through Llanymynech is currently unnavigable.

Llanymynech Rocks

The reserve lies at the southern end of the Carboniferous limestone outcrop that stretches from Anglesey and the Great Orme in Llandudno. Until the end of the First World War the site was a busy limestone quarry. The lime-rich soil gives the reserve its character, particularly the grassland and wildflowers that have taken over the quarry floor and spoil tips. The amphitheatre is a bright with colour and alive with butterflies – Pearl Bordered Fritillary, the Grizzled Skipper, the Dingy Skipper, Grayling, and Wall Brown. It is designated as an SSSI. There is trad. rock climbing here and multi-pitch VS classics of 55m, and more recent developments of 7a routes. In all there are about 125 routes in 10 different areas. Climbing is restricted between 1 March-30 June to protect nesting birds.

Day 11 Llanymynech to Chirk

Wednesday 22 June (14 miles)

An early start at 7am. On the road a sign about a young Charles Darwin visited here in July 1831 to use his clinometer. This measures angles or inclination with respect to the horizontal. Darwin started his geological study in Pen-y-Foel cutting where he was learning how to use his instruments before touring North Wales with Prof Adam Sedgwick, Cambridge Professor of Geology. Darwin was appointed naturalist adviser on HMS Beagle later that year.

The path climbs to the quarries. The first is very like Venezuelan sandstone, but further on the rock is whiter, Carboniferous limestone. Llanymynech Hill forms a distinctive ridge and the imposing limestone cliffs can be seen for miles. Fossilised seashells and corals can be found here, as well as rare plants. The Romans mined here for copper and lead and the Carboniferous limestone was quarried for lime burning.

There is a view across the floodplains of the River Severn. Song of the

Llanymyneck Rocks

> **Tanat Valley Light Railway**
>
> The Tanat Valley light railway and the Nant Mawr branch is a restoration project. The Tanat Valley Light Railway (TVLR) was a 15-mile (24 km) long standard gauge light railway. It ran westwards from Llanyblodwel in Shropshire up the Tanat valley, terminating at Llangynog in the Berwyns. It opened in 1904, providing access to a remote area.

Chitchat. Then a lovely shady walk through woods. I go wrong at the golf course, retrace my steps, and cut up an overgrown path and soon find the forest trail which descends to the valley. A chicken factory with solar panels. A redundant rail line and a sign saying a group is trying to reinstate it.

There is more road through Nant Mawr. There is a cottage called Mount Zion where the road ends and Jones's Rough begins and a sign saying that it is a rewilding project. In a glade there is a delightful, abandoned, tiny one-room house, with a ladder to a sleeping platform. A crude table and bench under an ancient tree in the yard.

Tanat Valley Light Railway

Abandoned house in Jones' Rough

Huge roots of ancient lime trees grabbing the Dyke with their woody claws.

Blackcap singing its heart out, then a climb to a viewpoint above Trefonen. From here I can see the rest of the Clwyds that I'll be walking the next couple of days. A leafy lane and a postie delivering to post boxes. A huge lime tree and a pleasant walk into Trefonen where the pub is closed till 5pm, so I go back to the post office and have a coffee and orange juice.

I thought I'd been going well but am distressed to discover I am only a third of the way to Chirk – such a long way to go still. I was just thinking no more Dyke when there it was right next to me. A clear limestone stream and I enter Candy Woods. The Dyke is quite evident, and someone has built a crude stone arbor and I lunch on pumpernickel bread and goats' cheese to the persistent call of a Chiff-Chaff. Huge roots of ancient lime trees grabbing the Dyke with their woody claws. The Dyke is green and verdant the whole way – woven with ancient trees, redolent of bird song. Sheep sounding in the distance down the slope. The Dyke is a sliver of peace and tranquility in a disturbed world. It's tempting to think the whole country is like this, this healthy, but it isn't, and it should be.

Walking such long distances, you get a strange mixed sense of power and fragility. Looking back miles and miles across paler and paler lines of hills, you get an immense feeling of energy and potency being able to traverse such

Bench in loving memory of Anne and Bill Park

Oswestry Racecourse

The Oswestry Racecourse Grandstand was built in 1804 and incorporated an umpire's box that provided refreshment for those who could afford a ticket, which generally meant the nobility. In its heyday, Oswestry races were well attended and there was much betting. Race weeks were lively affairs with balls and festivities, but by the 1840s outsiders from the lower classes were winning prizes and rowdy behaviour caused attendances to fall. In 1848 the course was abandoned, and the grandstand fell into ruin.

distances, yet you know your body is weak and puny and you're tired and aching. A bench in memory of an Anne and Bill Park.

I get to Oswestry Racecourse on top of Cym y Bwch. Once a huge annual event, now all gone, but for the ruin of the grandstand and the outline of the course in the clover and buttercups. The cottage, where the chains for closing the road were stored, is still here, tranquil, and beautiful.

Descent on a track to Craignant. A friendly policeman waves to me as he drives past, and I stop briefly for an apple and a rest. A grass avenue climbs to

Remains of Oswestry Racecourse Grandstand

the Dyke, more ascent, then a deep ravine with steep, dangerous wooden steps and a steep slope with tree roots that need navigating. This walk keeps giving!

As I reach the main road at Chirk Mill a woman is just leaving her house and is about to get into her car, a green Jag. 'Hello', I say, 'is there a bus into Chirk?' 'I don't know if it's gone, but I can give you a lift; I'm going to the station.' She moves stuff around on the back seat to make room for me. She says her name is Heather and she's always lived around here, previously higher up the hill, with horses, now all gone. The interesting thing is that although her accent is clearly Welsh it also has a Scouse twang. I'd always suspected that the Liverpudlian accent owed a lot to Welsh but couldn't square this idea with the soft South Welsh accent one hears on TV. She also has mannerisms and speech patterns that remind me of Liverpudlians.

She delivers me to the door of my hotel – the Hand in Chirk. I have a huge room with an equally huge, but rather uncomfortable, bed. Dinner is a delicious tomato chickpea, potato and veg soup followed by a tuna ciabatta. They make me a packed lunch to take tomorrow as I hope to leave by 6am.

Steep wooden steps descending to Chirk Mill

Chirk, Y Waun (4500)

Two families are associated with the town and castle: the Trevor and Myddelton families. Chirk Castle is medieval and Chirk was formerly a coal mining community, with coal being worked from the 17th to the 20th century. These coal mines have now closed. The Llangollen branch of the Shropshire Union Canal runs through Chirk. Kronospan lumber runs the large factory in the town making chipboard and MDF. Cadbury also has a factory processing cocoa beans.

Hand Hotel, Chirk

Day 12 Chirk to Llandegla

Thursday 23 June (16 miles)

I depart the silent hotel soon after 5.30am to a clear bright morning and to the oppressive noise from the huge timber factory that kept me awake last night. I can hear the cacophony of lorries loading and machinery as I join the shady, pale tranquility of the canal and continue my walk north. Tranquil now, but the canal once brought industry, noise, and dirt. A man fishing off the prow of his narrow boat. People in pajamas making tea. Mallard mums with ducklings, birdsong.

A long tunnel, the domed light at the end reflected to make a complete oval. Walking in the dark. Good that there's a handrail since my balance is not great.

A narrow boat passes me as I'm sitting on a bench for a quick rest. Amazingly, I catch it up and pass it and get to Froncysylite, where a boat is going through the swing bridge. No problem, I'd already decided to take the alternative route over Telford's Pontcysyllte aqueduct.

Whitehouse Tunnel, Llangollen Canal

Narrow boat on Llangollen Canal at Froncysylite

Telford's Pontcysyllte aqueduct. (1805)

Llangollen Canal

Going south, the Chirk Tunnel is a quarter of mile long and has room for only one boat at a time. Going north, the canal passes through the 175 metres long Whitehouse Tunnel to cross the Valley of the Dee at Pontcysyllite, where Thomas Telford's aqueduct (1795-1805) carries boats 120 feet above the river. The canal contains many fish including Roach, Dace, and Gudgeon.

Footbridge over the Llangollen Canal

The aquaduct soars hundreds of feet above the River Dee, a handrail on one side and nothing on the other. Must be amazing to cross on a narrow boat. Lead lined, with a strong flow towards Chirk. And below me the River Dee. I know the mudflats of the estuary on the other side of the Wirral, from birdwatching trips, but I haven't given the river the regard it's due. The ancient Britons referred to the Dee as Devos, or Mother Goddess, the 'mother of all rivers'. In modern Welsh, she is Dyfrdwy, 'the waters of the goddess'.

At Pontcysyllte the canal bends west towards Llangollen and I cross by an iron bridge with a stone bed, worn smooth by many feet. A gentle rising traverse through the woods of the Trevor estate. Birdsong – Wren, Jay, Tree Creeper, Blue Tit, and Great Tit. At this time of the year the Dyke is a continual river of birdsong, a symphony to nature, seemingly endless.

The panorama road is beautiful but hard on the feet. I'm nearly at Worlds End. I came here to climb in the 1960s with Malcolm Hodgins, my friend from school and university. We also came caving near here, at Loggerheads, just east of where I'll be walking tomorrow on the Clwydian Range. We went caving when we were teenagers at school and my caving equipment consisted of a bike lamp, clamped to my forehead with the belt from my gabardine mackintosh. Contouring the narrow, precipitous path, half a dozen Redstarts;

Trevor Rocks and Castle Dinas Bran, Panorama Road, Creigiau Eglwyseg

russet breast, black cap with white flash singing twit twit, click click click.

I stop for lunch at Worlds End, where the stream crosses the road in a ford. I take off my boots and paddle. The sandwich, tuna on white, I eat sitting on a rock with my feet in the stream, and my bottle of water and orange cooling in the cold limestone water.

A hard pull up the road onto the moor. Stonechat singing in the heather. I'm looking out for the footpath. The OS map GPS says I'm there, but I don't think so, because, although there's a path, there is no sign and there should be one. So, I stop for an apple and to reflect. Then I walk on 100 yards and find a big sign and a stone slab path that runs all the way to the forest. It's incredibly well-laid, level and stable. I stop at the edge of the woods for a quick break. Soon after, in the middle of the track in the hot sun, a brown and black bootlace that moves and I realise it is an Adder, before it slips away and disappears into the bracken.

Stone path across Llandegla Moor

A walk through the woods on pine needles and a descent past a house with colonnades. Unbelievably I go wrong again following a nice green path. I realise I'm wrong and try climbing the hill to spot the way. There is a modern electric fence in the way and rather than climb back, I use the rubber grips on my poles to hold the wire down while I hop over. Into the village and the community cafe and shop. It's delightful – cool and wholesome and offering delightful refreshment. An elderly foursome is having a monster cream tea. I order a pot of tea and a scone with cream and jam, and a Fentiman's lemonade.

The Raven Hotel in Llanarmon is also a community enterprise. I sit outside, waiting for it to open at five. I rang Malcom and asked him about climbing at World's End. He tells me that we came here when we were at university and, although I have no memory of it, we trundled a massive boulder that smashed into a farmer's fence after rolling down the hill. Liverpudlian hooligans! Dangerous, thoughtless, stupid. I've blotted it from my memory. Malcolm said he couldn't remember if it was my idea or his.

Tea at the community cafe in Llandegla

Llandegla (600)

Llandegla named from the 13th century Church of Saint Tecla, a Welsh virgin. Located on a main drovers' road and was noted by Pennant for its vast fairs of black cattle. Sufferers of St Tecla's disease (epilepsy) washed themselves in the church well, walked round the church three times and spent the night in the church. The local cafe is in a community shop.

Llanarmon-yn-Ial (1000)

The village is considered the capital of the community of Iâl (Yale), the "fertile hill country". The village grew up around St Garmon's shrine. Like Llandegla it was located on various drovers' roads coming from Anglesey to England over the Clwydian Range.

Raven Hotel, Llanarmon

Day 13 Llanarmon to Bodfari

Friday 24 June (18 miles)

Away by 6am to a beautiful, fresh new day. Sunlight on the church stone wall. A long steady pull up to the ridge and the Offa's Dyke Path, which skirts the next big top of Moel Fenlli. I lost my water bottle when I threw my sac down, then found a better one twenty minutes later.
Breakfast, and a farmer's wife arrives at the stile I'm sitting on. I do this walk every day with my two dogs Pip and Jack, she says. Her name is Edith. Born in Abergele, daughter of farmer, trained as a theatre nurse in Liverpool. 'We have 300 sheep and a caravan site next to the pond you can see over there', she says, pointing into the valley. 'We used to do B&B, but it all went online.' I ask about the farming economy. 'It's all uncertain', she says. 'Boris – he'll have to go, she says, after losing Tiverton and Wakefield.'

Each day, by mid-morning, I feel I've gone a long way and am doing so well that I'll finish early, soon after lunch. But the day goes on, and I get tired and go

Morning light on St Garmon's Church, Llanarmon

slower and end up doing 2 miles an hour or a bit less.

Pine trees downed like pickup sticks in the recent storm. I go wrong and have to climb over a fence. On through rolling green hills and heather with a steep climb then a descent to Bwlch Penbarra car park, where the road crosses the range. The track contours round, avoiding the top. Suddenly there are lots of people, walkers, and joggers and three talkative ladies with whippet dogs, all climbing the slope to Moel Fanau and the Jubilee Tower.

More up and down to Moel Arthur, the hillfort. Chillier now. Three meadow pipits dancing, seemingly playing in the ridge lift. Orange-tipped butterflies.

An excellent publication entitled "Heather and Hillforts" talks about the natural and historic heritage of the Clwydian Range and Llantysilio Mountains[1].

During the final glaciation that ended 10,000 years ago, the area was affected by ice streams from Snowdonia and from the Irish Sea Ice that rounded the relatively soft mudstones and created the rolling hills we see today. Erratics of

---

[1] Heather and Hillforts of the Clwydian Range and Llantysilio Mountains (2011) Heather and Hillforts Partnership Board, Denbighshire County Council

Edith walking her dogs

Jubillee Tower Moel Fanau

Moel Arthur hill fort

> **Jubillee Tower Moel Fanau**
>
> The Jubilee Tower on the top of Moel Famau is the highest built structure in Northeast Wales at 554m. The tower was built to celebrate the 50-year reign of George III (Mad King George). Over 3000 people gathered in their best clothes to see the foundation stone laid in 1810. Work stopped after a huge row in 1815 between Harrison, the architect and Penson, the builder. By 1846 the tower was already crumbling, and the obelisk collapsed suddenly after a storm. The base has become a familiar landmark.

volcanic rock from near Bala have been found all over the Clwydian Range and rocks Scotland and the Lake District rocks reached Shrewsbury.

People have exploited the lie of the land, building forts on hilltops, and quarrying the stone. I now regret not having done my homework and for not paying more attention to burial sites and hillforts as I walked. I walked right across Penycloddiau, one of the largest Iron-Age hillforts in Britain, just north of Moel Arthur, without even realising. Nor did I note any of the burial mounds. Until the Romans arrived, metal tools were rare, and hillforts were constructed using antler picks and shoulder blades of oxen. Imagine the labour involved in digging the deep ditches, some from solid rock. Now they merge into the landscape, and all that remains is the trace of the surrounding ditches. But originally, they would have been towering stone-walled ramparts topped by a timber palisade and imposing gatehouses. Penycloddiau enclosed 21 hectares, had a double rampart and required over 10,00 trees for posts, beams and planks to build the palisade. It is hard to imagine how awe-inspiring they

> **Moel Arthur Hillfort**
>
> The earth banks and ditches of the Iron Age hill fort were made over 2000 years ago. The steep southern edge has a single rampart while the gentle sloping northern side has a larger double rampart. The people were farmers growing grain and pulses and keeping sheep cattle and pigs. They lived in wooden framed roundhouses with a central hearth. They coppiced woodland to grow poles for building, forged iron and worked bronze.

would have been, and how effective in intimidating and enslaving an indigenous population. The largest would have had a similar social impact to that of a Medieval cathedral and as well as providing defence and deterring attack, they marked the status of the clan chief.

Bodari is beautiful, set at the foot of tree-covered bluff. But you wouldn't see this if you drove past on the main road. It isn't easy to find my B&B because the postcode doesn't take me to the right place and when I finally arrive, my host, Ian Priestley, explains that he was out, and the reception died when he was trying to direct me. Ian asked if I had booked a table at the local pub, the Dinorben Arms. I haven't. Ian tries ringing, and I say, 'this is cheeky, but could you possibly do me of an evening breakfast'. He grins and says it will cost an arm and a leg. 'It's a seller's market', I tell him.

Bodfari (300)

The village lies on the A541 Mold road where it passes through a gap in the Clwydian Hills, where the River Wheeler cuts through the range. Offa's Dyke and the Clwydian Way pass through the village.

Fron-haul, above Bodfari

St Stephen's Church, Bodfari

Day 14 Bodfari to Prestatyn

Saturday 25 June (12 miles)

A long sleep, then woken by bird song. A cooked breakfast and real coffee. Ian's wife is lovely and friendly. Ian built the house himself and they're well set up with solar panels, wall chargers, Tesla, and Leaf cars. A great place to stay.

A few people, like Ian, seem to have moved out here and got permission to demolish old farmhouses and rebuild. All the new houses have slate stone gateposts and ornate steel gates with keypad entry, cameras etc. Cool south wind and the rolling last gasp of the Clwyds. Great views of the coast and the Snowden Range. I find a car key from a VW in the grass. Someone's dropped it. It has mud on it, and it looks as though it been here a couple of days. I debate what to do and decide to leave it on the stile.

This area of North Wales is so beautiful. It was my stamping ground as a child from the age of nine or ten. We used to come to Llandudno for holidays and we drove along the coast, past Prestatyn and Rhyl. Later, when we started

Cliff path above Prestatyn

going to Borth-y-Gest, we'd drive this way through Ruthin. But I'm ashamed to say that I didn't appreciate the countryside, as it deserves. Maybe I took it for granted, or maybe I was already dreaming of faraway places, bigger mountains, and more exotic cultures. Maybe North Wales was too like home. Or, most likely, I didn't see it properly from a moving car. Yet later, as a teenager, I used to cycle out this far from Liverpool. It must have had an effect, an influence. Maybe you must walk the country lanes and green pastures, like I've been doing the last few days, to begin to really see and appreciate.

The Dyke doesn't give out or disappoint. I'd imagined it to be all flat from here, but not a bit of it. The route follows the line of the Clwyd Hills with ups and downs, past pleasant limestone escarpments and finishes in a traverse along the cliffs above Prestatyn. I can see lots of wind turbines out at sea. A walk through the town. The post outside the Nova Centre says Start – Finish but it's still a short walk to the beach to sand and sea.

Then a walk back into town to the bus station. Passing a taxi office and get a taxi to the Berwyn Guesthouse in Rhyl and the end of my walk.

I feel pleased and satisfied I've done the walk in good style. I am tired and a bit sore but not unduly and feel that I could keep going. It has been easier

High Street, Prestatyn

without the camping gear and food. I've been ill with Covid, but only really found it tough in the steep Shropshire Hills, from Knucklas to Montgomery.

Offa's Dyke is one of the great walks, better and more interesting than I'd expected and well worth doing.

Prestatyn (19,000)

There has been a settlement on this site since pre-history and there was a Roman fort and bathhouse here on the road from Chester to Caernarfon. The name derives from the Old English prēosta (priests' place). There was a Norman castle here, destroyed by the Welsh in 1167. For centuries it was a fishing village until the arrival of the railway in the 19th century turned it into a holiday destination. "Sunny Prestatyn" became famous for its beach, clean seas, and promenade entertainers. The UK's first major offshore wind farm was opened in Liverpool Bay, 5 miles off the coast of Prestatyn in 2003. There are now dozens of wind turbines.

Start – Finish post, Prestatyn

Author on Hatterall Hill, Black Mountains

OFFA'S DYKE

Offa's Dyke path can be divided into 5 sections, all quite different in character, and this variety makes the walk much more interesting and enjoyable. It also means that some parts are more up and down than others, one of the primary considerations on a long-distance path. But despite the hard work, the hilly bits are the best bits because of the views. It is 177 miles (285 km) long and runs between the Severn Estuary in the south and Liverpool Bay in the north. I walked it in 12 days.

Offa's Dyke (Clawdd Offa) is a linear earthwork named after Offa, the Anglo-Saxon king of Mercia (AD 757-796), who is traditionally believed to have ordered its construction. Although its precise purpose is unknown, it delineated the border between Anglian Mercia and the Welsh kingdom of Powys. It was customary for the English to cut off the ears of every Welshman who was found to the east of the dyke, and for the Welsh to hang every Englishman whom they found to the west of it.

The earthwork traverses low ground, hills, and rivers. Although the Dyke has conventionally been dated to the Early Middle Ages of Anglo-Saxon England, radioactive carbon dating shows that it was started in the early 5th century, during the sub-Roman period.

Today it is protected as a scheduled monument and some sections are also defined as Sites of Special Scientific Interest, including stretches within the Lower Wye Valley SSSI and the Highbury Wood National Nature Reserve. The Wye Valley, Shropshire Hills and the Clwydian Range are Areas of Outstanding Natural Beauty. Most of the line of Offa's Dyke is designated as a public right of way, including those sections which form part of the Offa's Dyke Path.

Length 82-150 miles. Width 20m (66 ft) including ditch; Height 2.5m

Drone shot of the Dyke south from Llanfair Hill towards Cwmsanahan Hill (Julian Ravest)

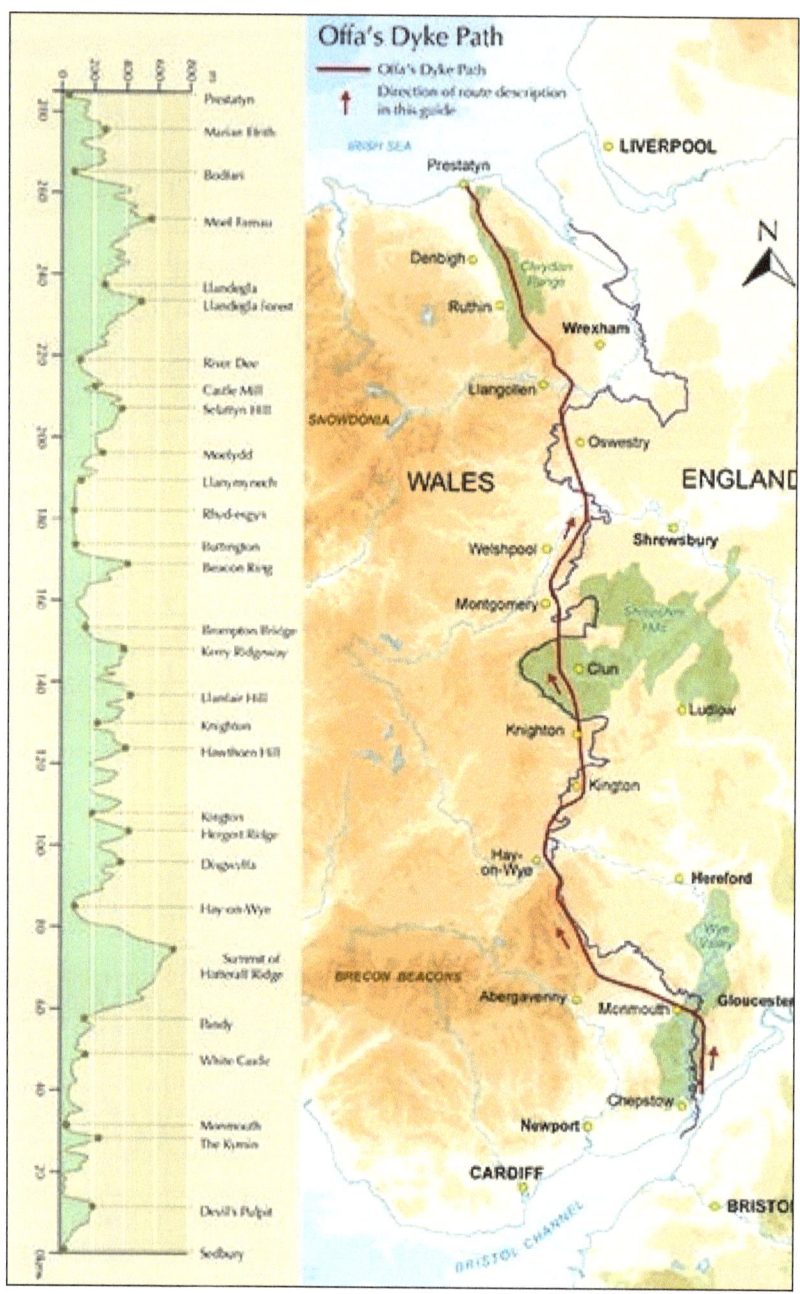

Offa's Dyke Path, Cicerone Guide

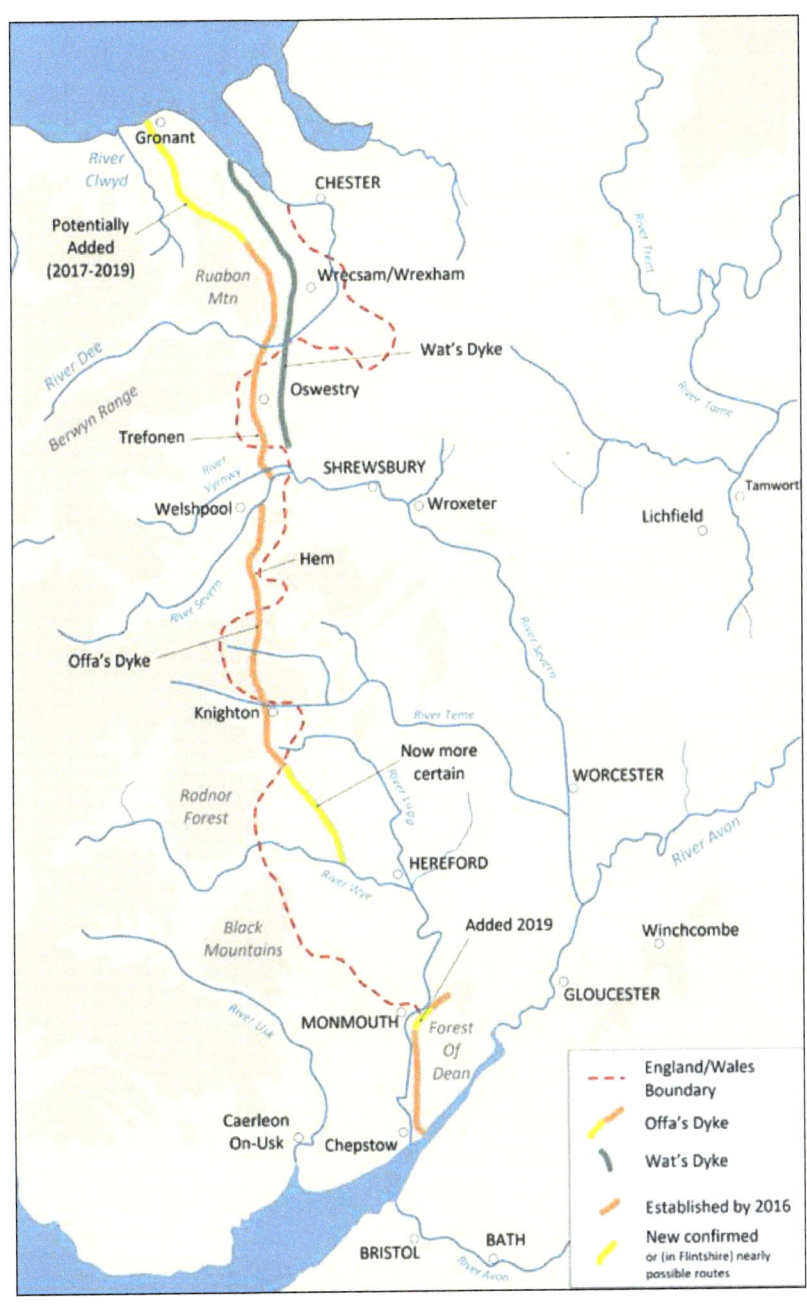

Offa's Dyke and Wat's Dyke (field reconnaissance 2017-2020. Map Simon Mayes)

ITINERARY

No.	Day	Date	Start	Finish	Km	Miles	Ht m	Accommodation
1	Sun	12-Jun	Chepstow	Chepstow	6	4		Woodfield House
2	Mon	13-Jun	Chepstow	Brockweir	15	9		Woodfield House
3	Tue	14-Jun	Brockweir	Monmouth	15	9	1100	Punch House
4	Wed	15-Jun	Monmouth	Pandy	26	16	580	Old Pandy Inn
5	Thu	16-Jun	Pandy	Hay-on-Wye	26	16	760	The Swan
6	Fri	17-Jun	Hay-on-Wye	Kington	24	15	690	Burton Hotel
7	Sat	18-Jun	Kington	Knighton	21.5	13	780	Castle Inn
8	Sun	19-Jun	Knucklas	Montgomery	30	19	1050	Dragon Hotel
9	Mon	20-Jun	Montgomery	Buttington	13.5	8	510	Royal Oak Welshpool
10	Tue	21-Jun	Welshpool	Llanymynech	17.5	11	90	Cross Keys Hotel
11	Wed	22-Jun	Llanymynech	Chirk	22.5	14	820	Hand Hotel
12	Thu	23-Jun	Chirk	Llandegla	25	16	915	Raven Inn
13	Fri	24-Jun	Llanarmon	Bodfari	29	18	1090	Lletr Eos
14	Sat	25-Jun	Bodfari	Prestatyn	20	12	670	Berwyn GH Rhyl
	TOTAL				291	180	9055	

There is a small discrepancy between my measurement of the distance covered of 180 miles and the usually accepted distance 177 miles. The difference is because I walked to and from Chepstow to the start of the walk at Sedbury and also walked to Tintern Abbey.

KIT LIST

Item	Make	Model	Notes	No.	Weight gm	Stars
Rucksack	Lightwave	Fastpac 30	Excellent, durable but very light. Could do with larger side pockets	1	993	***
First aid kit			Good, added compeed, second skin, arnica,	1	123	***
Note book	Moleskin		I always use this make for my journals	1	111	***
Pens	Biro		Excellent	2	22	***
Phone	iPhone	12	Good battery life, excellent camera	1	75	***
Battery/cable	Anker	72 wh	Excellent	1	343	***
Maps	Cicerone	Offa's Dyke Path	Excellent, very accurate, durable and easy to use	2	46	***
Compass	Silva	with whistle	Excellen, very practical, have always used Silva	1	42	***
Debit card			Essential	1	1	
Dry bags	Sea to Summit	Assorted	Excellent, durable and completely waterproof	5	310	***
Walking poles	Black Diamond	Distance flz	Excellent, light and well balanced	2	384	***
Sandals	Clogs		Useful in camp for tired feet and for getting water from streams	1	296	**
Oat bars	Trek		Excellent energy giving snack	4	96	***
Lip salve	Soltan	factor 30		1	7	
Sun cream	Nivea	Sun 30		1	45	
Toothpaste	Colgate			1	15	
Toothbrush	CuraProX			1	10	
Contact lenses				1	12	
Spectacles				1	70	
Eye drops				1	9	
TOTAL KIT					3,010	
Boots	Meindl	Bhutan	Excellent, especially for wider feet	1	1,964	***
Gaiters	Sea to Summit		Good, light	1	110	**
Anorak	Arcteryx	Alpha SV	Orange	1	506	***
Fleece	Berghaus		Windproof with hood	1	518	***
Overtousers	Beghaus	Gortex Paclite	Used	1	192	***
Cap	North face		Excellent, old friend	1	86	***
Pants	Kühl		Excellent, fit well and good pockets	1	351	***
Shorts	Haglofs		Excellent, fit well and good pockets	1	299	***
T shirts	Adidas		Excellent, stayedlooking smart	1	150	***
Inner socks	Bridgedale		Excellent, very comfortable	2	104	**
Outer socks	Bridgedale		Excellent, very comfortable	2	0	***
Underpants	M&S			2	46	
Belt	Jukmo	Ratchet belt	Essential, because you loose weight (6-7 kilos)	1	25	
TOTAL CLOTHES					4,351	
TOTAL					7,361	

TRAINING WALKS

Date	Name	Mileage	Km	Ht ft	Time hrs
04/01/22	Stanage Edge, Peak	3.4	5.4	656	2
05/01/22	Crook Hill Fairholms, Peak	7.8	12.5	656	4
12/01/22	Cuthroat Bridge, Derwent Edge, Peak	7.3	11.8	787	3
14/01/22	Lose Hill, Peak	6.8	11.0	984	3
22/01/22	Dunsop, Brennand, Trough of Bowland	9.8	15.7	1148	5
23/01/22	Fair Snape Fell, Bowland	10.5	16.9	1558	6
08/02/22	Ward's Stone, Bowland	11.0	17.7	1864	6
09/02/22	Clougha Pike	5.0	8.0	1148	3
10/02/22	Ingleborough from Clapham, Dales	11.0	17.7	1841	5
23/02/22	White Edge, Peak	3.2	5.2	33	2
09/03/22	The Dale, Hathersage	3.9	6.2	328	2
20/03/22	Three Shires Head, Peak	7.3	11.7	656	3
26/03/22	Combe Edge, Castle Naze, Peak	3.4	5.5	591	2
09/04/22	Cautley Spout & Calf, Yorkshire Dales	10.5	16.9	2644	6
10/04/22	Great Whernside, Yorkshire Dales	8.0	12.9	1821	6
23/4/22	Bradford Dale, Lathkill Dale	8.5	13.7	755	4
26/04/22	New Road Stoney Middleton Eyam, Peak	3.7	6.0	328	3
24/05/22	Hebden Dale, Hardcastle Crags	3.9	6.3	100	3
25/05/22	Heptonstall Moor, Raistrick Greave	10.4	16.8	492	5
26/05/22	Colden Clough, Heptonstall	2.9	4.6	164	2
	Total	139	222	18,555	75

TRAINING WALKS

BERWYNS AND LLANTYSILIO MOUNTAIN

29-30 July

Fresh from Offa's Dyke, and I'm back in North Wales to walk in the Berwyns, about 15 miles due west of Oswestry Racecourse, and on Llantysilio Mountain, 2 miles northwest of Llangollen. Although I've been past them both many times on the way to Snowdonia on the A5, I don't know them and have never walked here. I feel I want to better appreciate this part of North Wales and there is no better way to do that than by walking. Last minute there was little available accommodation and the nearest I could find was in Oswestry.

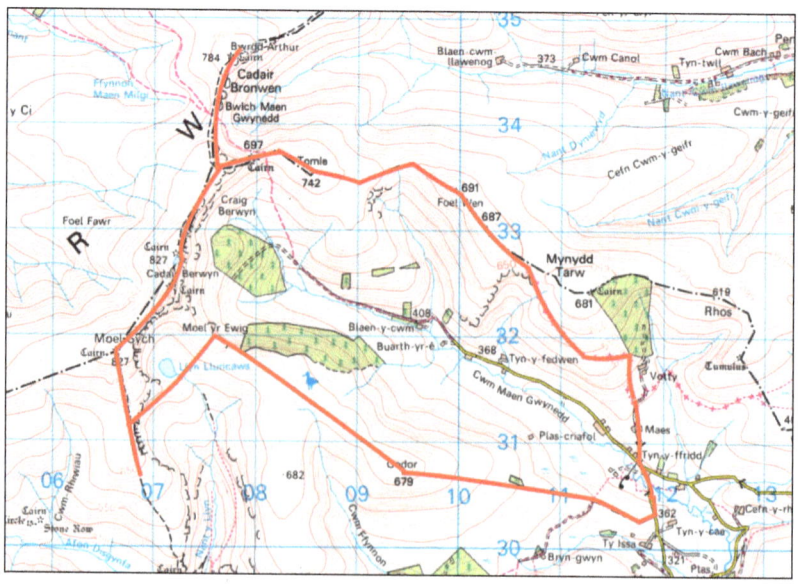

Berwins Route, 11 miles (18 km) Ascent 842m (2763 ft)

THE BERWYNS

The Berwyns are an isolated and sparsely populated area of moorland. They are not that popular with hillwalkers since the peaks are lower than those in nearby Snowdonia. Consequently, one has the mountain practically to oneself. The topmost peaks are rugged, and the main summits are Cadair Berwyn at 832 metres (2,730 ft), Moel Sych at 827 metres (2,713 ft) and Cadair Bronwen at 783 metres (2,569 ft). The rock is sedimentary and similar to that on the Clwydian Range but has been subjected to volcanic action and glaciation.

The Berwyn Mountains are special in Celtic mythology as the geographical location of Annwn, the Celtic Otherworld, the place of the spirits of the dead in the land of the ancient Britons. Celts believed that the descendants of Dana, the life-giver, the daughter of the mother goddess Mathonwy, were the Lords of Annwn. The Otherworld is a kingdom ruled by Gwyn ap Nudd, king of the fairies or spirit folk and of the land of the dead. Legend has it that travelers crossing the moors of the Berwyns are sometimes invited to join in the feasting and dancing, but to choose to do so means they cannot return to the land of

The path up Tomle to the great ridge with Cadair Berwyn and Moel Sych to the left

the living. The only way to escape is to refuse to eat or drink.

Leaving Oswestry, Google found Tan-y Ffridd on the wrong side of the mountains and I ended up on a narrow farm track and had to turn round. I'd felt I was going wrong, but followed the Satnav blindly, enjoying pooterling along the country lanes and feeling in the mood to explore. The Tanat Valley to Llangynog and the spectacular road by Afon Eirth to Llandderfel were worth the extra mileage.

I'd plotted a circular walk on OS maps, that climbed the shoulder of Foel Wen and Tomle to the main ridge of the Berwyns. A nice woman at the Ysgol Outdoor Centre told me to park by the stream below Tyn-y-Ffridd. I set off up a track and then contoured to Mynydd Tarw and stopped for a late lunch in the soft heather and took off my boots. It was cloudy and chilly, so I didn't stop long. The way was clear, but the path across the peaty moorland indefinite and clearly not many people come this way. In contrast, the summit ridge from Cadair Bronwen in the north-east to Moel Sych in the south-west is well marked and trafficked and even has wooden staging across what are boggy sections in less dry conditions. There is a large shelter cairn on the summit of Cadair Berwyn in the form of a caracol that you can climb into.

Cadair Berwyn and Moel Sych

Much of the area is designated a national nature reserve and an SSSI and is one of the best moorland breeding bird areas south of the Scottish highlands, with Red Grouse, Black Grouse, Merlin, Hen Harrier, Buzzard, Red Kite, Peregrine falcon and Curlew.

I stop for coffee on the summit of Moel Sych and contemplate Llyn Llancaws, nestling in the cwm below, and wonder if this might be an alternative to returning along the ridge to Cadair Berwyn. Without thinking, I set off to "have a look" and in no time am committed. having descended 200 metres or so. There is a good track, but it leads south rather than east and would take me miles away from the car. I can see the ridge above me, but the vegetation looks too deep to wade through, and the only alternative is to go back, skirt the lake and hope there is a sheep track up Moel yr Ewig and the ridge. And so, it proves. There is no path on the top, clearly few people come this way, but the way down the ridge is clear over Godor to Tyn-y-Ffridd. A longer day than I'd anticipated, but I feel fine, with a renewed vigour having got off the beaten track. It feels like old times breaking away from the fixed path and chancing my arm.

Cadair Berwyn, Llyn Llancaws and Moel yr Ewig ridge

LLANTYSILIO MOUNTAIN

Llantysilio Mountain is a rugged upland landscape that provides a stark contrast with the green fields and woods of the valley of the River Dee to the south. The moorland is home to the rare black grouse, as well as other mountain birds such as the golden plover, ring ouzel and merlin. I'd driven past these hills many times on my way west but had never walked here. I drive to Llangollen and continue along the A5 to Glydyfridwy and take a narrow mountain road to just west of Moel Morfydd (549). It's misty today but it's impossible to get lost on the huge bridle track that crosses the range. Unfortunately, the views of Snowdonia and the Lakes from the trig point on the summit are hidden behind cloud.

There is evidence for human activity here dating back to at least the Bronze Age (2,000 BC) with a large burial cairn on the summit of Moel y Gamelin. During the Iron Age (1000 BC) Moel y Gaer was chosen as the site for a small hillfort. Again, I walk straight over the hillfort, without realising, being fixated by the mess the off-roaders have made on the col below Moel y Gamelin.

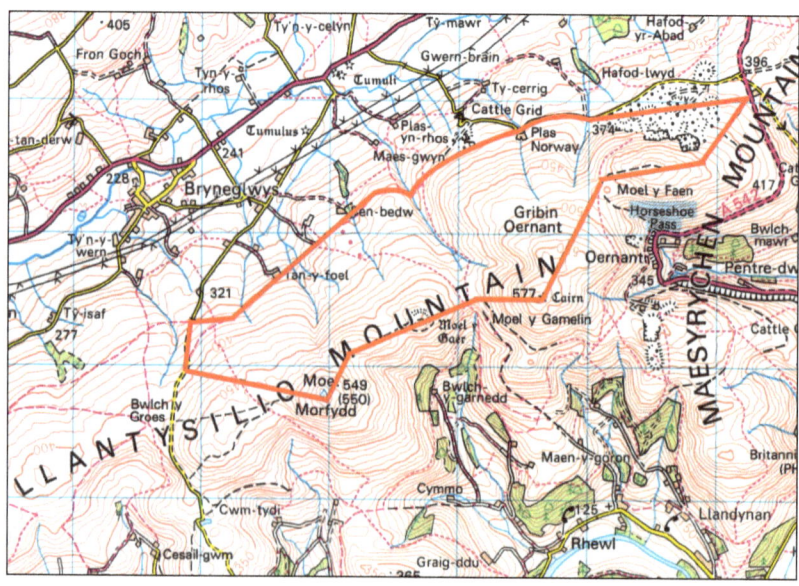

Llantysilio Mountain, Route 8 miles (13 km) Ascent 310 m (1020 ft)

From Moel y Faen the path continues down to the Ponderosa cafe complex on the Horseshoe Pass. I head into the quarry, looking into the old workings and on past the tips of sorted stone that reveal the geology of the area. At Plas Norway you have to climb a fence to gain the footpath that skirts the north side of the mountain. Clearly the farmers around here don't make life easy for walkers. Maybe I was right as a youth, sensing the antipathy to English city dwellers from people in this part of rural North Wales. Yet when I get back to the car a farmer on a quad bike with his dogs stops for a friendly chat and wishes me well.

Moel y Gaer hillfort, Llantysilio Mountain

Moel Morfydd

Avenue of ancient birch near Pen-y-cae, north of Moel Morfydd

The Story of Wales

The story begins over 400 million years ago with the northward migration of Wales from the southern hemisphere. The mudstones, siltstones and sandstones were once mud, silt and sand that were deposited in a deep sea called the Welsh Basin. A steady 'rain' of black mud accumulated on the sea floor. A month after I got back from Offa's Dyke, I walked along the ridge of the Llantysilio Mountains and could see the piles of stone from pale yellow to dark black in Moel-faen Quarries at the north-east end of the ridge. The report has a table of archaeological time periods from the Paleolithic (Old Stone Age) to the present and it struck me that Raymond Williams may have seen something similar and got the idea of imagining life in each time.
The landscape was re-shaped by glaciation over the last 2 million years. Bronze Age burial mounds that dot the hills. Penycloddiau has a Bronze Age barrow within the fort itself.

Hillforts of the Clwydian Range and Llantysilio Mountains

Neanderthal people lived in the Pontnewydd Cave over 200,00 years ago, just 4 miles west of Bodfari and Offa's Dyke. During the Upper Palaeolithic (25,000 year ago) people moved to high ground camps in the summer following the large herbivores – the deer elk and horses. They moved back to caves or to the coast in winter. These small bands of hunter-gatherers created glades in woodland to make it easier to hunt but had little effect on the landscape. During the Mesolithic (6000-10,000 years ago) this pattern of hunting and transhumance continued, but new people began to arrive by sea, bringing with them new ways and small flocks of sheep, and the people followed their grazing herds as they moved up and down the mountains. From 3000BC, farming increasingly transformed the land, and metals – copper, tin and lead – were mined from 2000BC. But the archaeological record is scant; so much has disappeared, organic objects are rare and only the most resistant materials remain. This is why Raymond Williams' imaginative recreation of life in the past is so evocative.

GEOLOGICAL MAP OF WALES

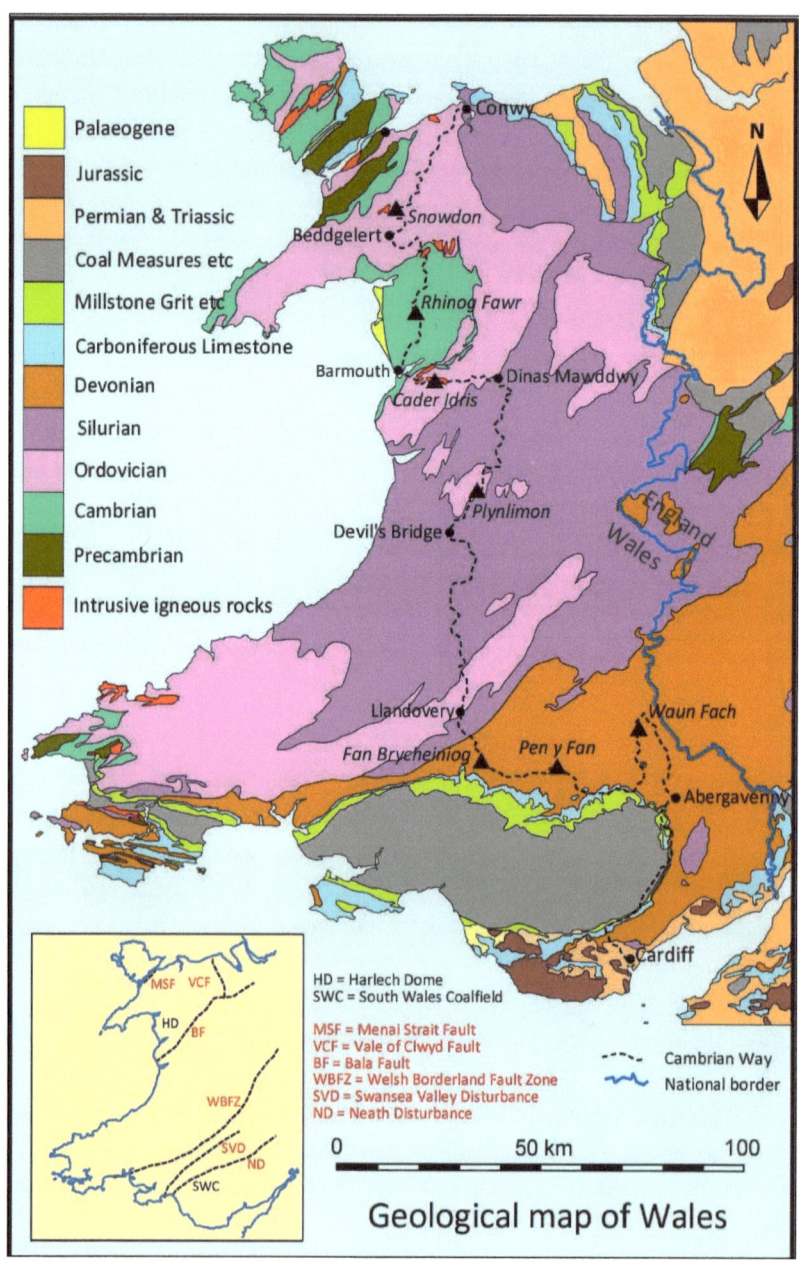

ARCHAEOLOGICAL TIME PERIODS

10000BC
9500BC
9000BC
8500BC
8000BC
7500BC
7000BC
6500BC
6000BC
5500BC
5000BC
4500BC
4000BC
3500BC
3000BC
2500BC
2000BC
1500BC
1000BC
500BC
0
AD500
AD1000
AD1500
AD2000

Pleistocene: about 1.64 million to about 8500BC
The first part of the geological Quaternary period, a time which included the ice ages appearance on earth of humans.

Palaeolithic (Old Stone Age): 220,000BC to 8500BC
The forbears of modern humans developed stone tools and lived a nomadic life following they hunted whilst also gathering food from plants. The oldest evidence of human activity in to about 220,000BC when Neanderthals lived in Pontnewydd Cave in modern Denbighsh humans had emerged by the end of the Palaeolithic.

Mesolithic (Middle Stone Age): 8500BC to 4000BC
The period between the end of the last Ice Age and the introduction of farming to the Briti was still nomadic, probably revolving around the changing seasons. People constructed shelters as they hunted animals with newly domesticated dogs, fished and collected foo coast and gathered berries, nuts and roots. The characteristic finds of this period are tiny flint called microliths.

Neolithic (New Stone Age): 4000BC to 2200BC
The Neolithic is defined by the domestication of plants and animals, the introduction of polished stone axes, and the construction of the first houses and monuments. Much forest cle place and great structures of stone and earth served as places of burial and the focus for lives of societies. Flint tools are the most commonly found artefacts dating to this time.

Bronze Age: 2200BC to 700BC
Societies that formerly relied solely on flint and stone as their main materials for makin weapons now began to use copper and bronze as well. Society itself seems to change in this a shift away from a focus on the group to that of the individual, hinted at by a move from burial to single burials or cremations. This may indicate the development of hierarchies in the migration of people or new ideas from the continent. There is also evidence of greater for the control of land.

Iron Age: 700BC to AD43
The first use of iron occurs in this period, complementing the older bronze working tech rearing of livestock seems to have been particularly important at this time when we see the of tribes controlling particular areas of Britain. The most easily recognisable site of this p hillfort, a defended village and stronghold and in some places the centre for metalworkin crafts. On lower ground farmsteads defended with banks and ditches topped by tin (palisades), in the manner of hillforts, were also occupied.

Roman: AD43 to AD410
The Romans arrived in Britain in AD43 and the conquest of Wales was completed by AD77. over Britain lasted for nearly 400 years, the army being withdrawn to defend territories on th in AD410. A series of forts linked by a network of roads was constructed to exert of the province.

Early Medieval: AD410 to 1086
Also known as the Dark Ages and the Age of the Saints and spanning the period between the of Roman rule and the Norman Conquest. Christianity spread and the kingdoms and l Wales. Little is known of settlement although some Iron Age hillforts were reoccupied. The and iconic remains are carved stone memorials to individuals, with writing in Latin a Ogham alphabet.

Medieval: AD1086 to 1536
The Normans imposed a new weapon, the castle, soon copied by the Welsh Princes as the invaders, and each other. In its earliest form this was a mound of earth (the motte) topped w tower and often supported by an enclosure surrounded by a bank and ditch (the bailey castle developed from this and became increasingly complex over succeeding centuries where markets could be controlled and taxed were established outside castles and soon grev

Post-Medieval: AD1536 to 1899
The beginning of the suppression of the monasteries by Henry VIII and the first Act of Ur Wales to England occurred in 1536 and mark the beginning of the Post-Medieval Period. Ma castles were reused defensively for the last time during the Civil War between 1642 and 16 advent of the Industrial Revolution in the 18th century (1700s) massive change came to economy, formerly dominated by agriculture, developed industrially and commercially a expanded greatly in size.

Modern: AD1900 to the present
Wales has experienced two World Wars and the collapse of the heavy and extractive indu 1945 the productivity and efficiency of farming has greatly expanded although the number o people working on them has decreased. The landscape has been altered by the construc farms, hydroelectric schemes and the planting of conifer forests in the uplands. The cou also had to adapt to the pressures of recreation, while towns have continued to expand threats to their historic character.

Taken from *Archwilio*, the Welsh Archaeological Trusts' Online Historic Enviro

ROMAN BRITAIN 150 AD

BRITAIN 500 AD

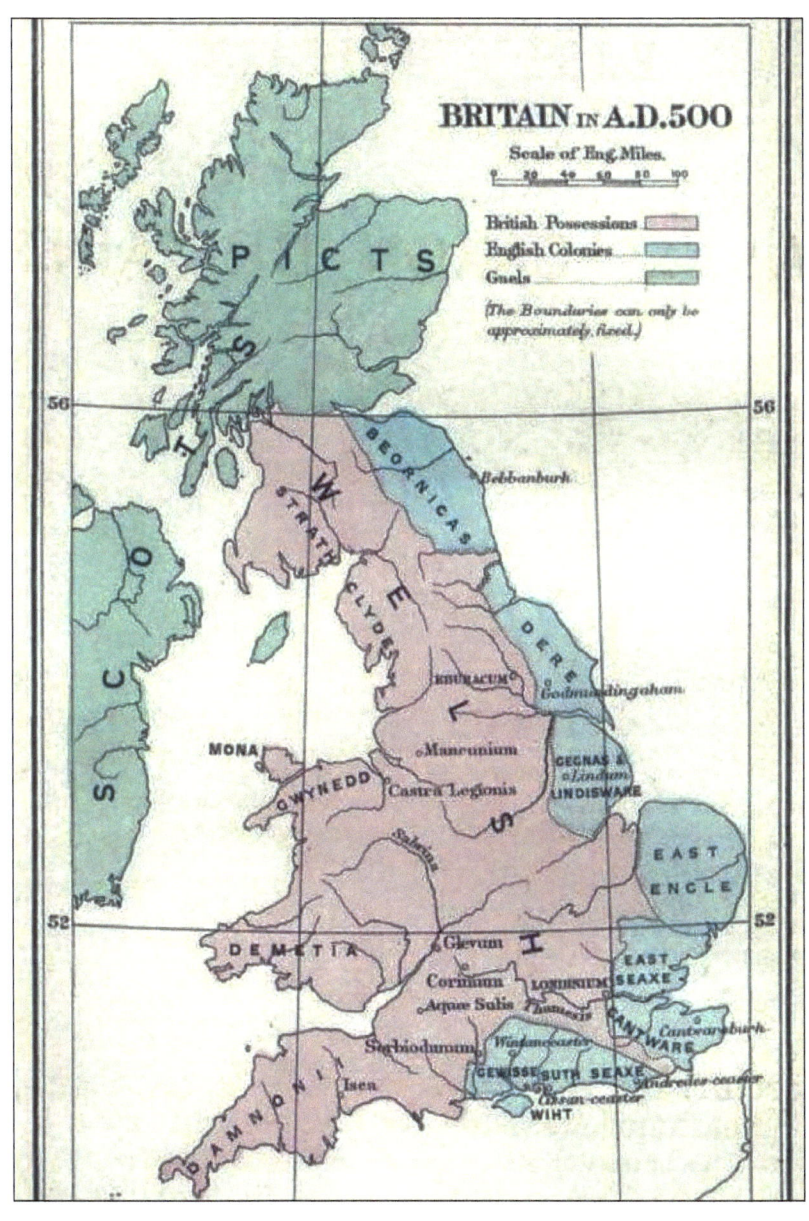

ANGLO-SAXON KINGDOMS 800 AD

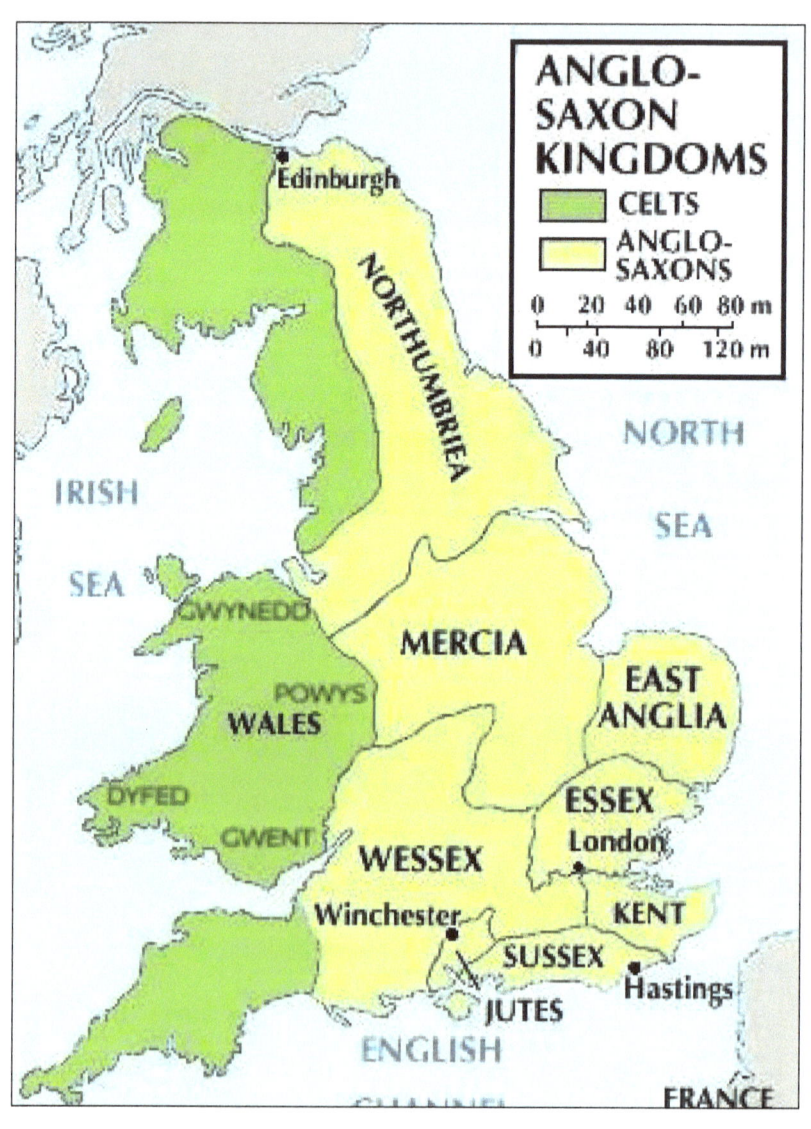

BRITAIN ON EVE OF NORMAN INVASION (1066)

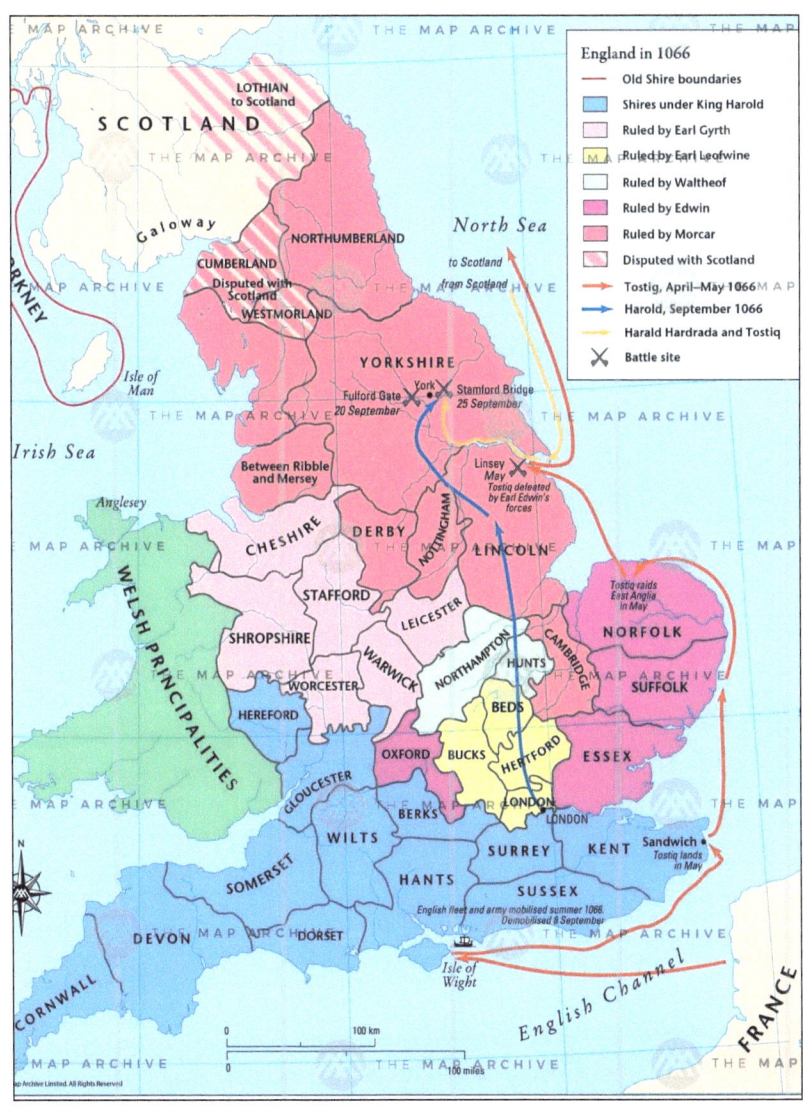

HISTORIC WELSH COUNTIES (1974)

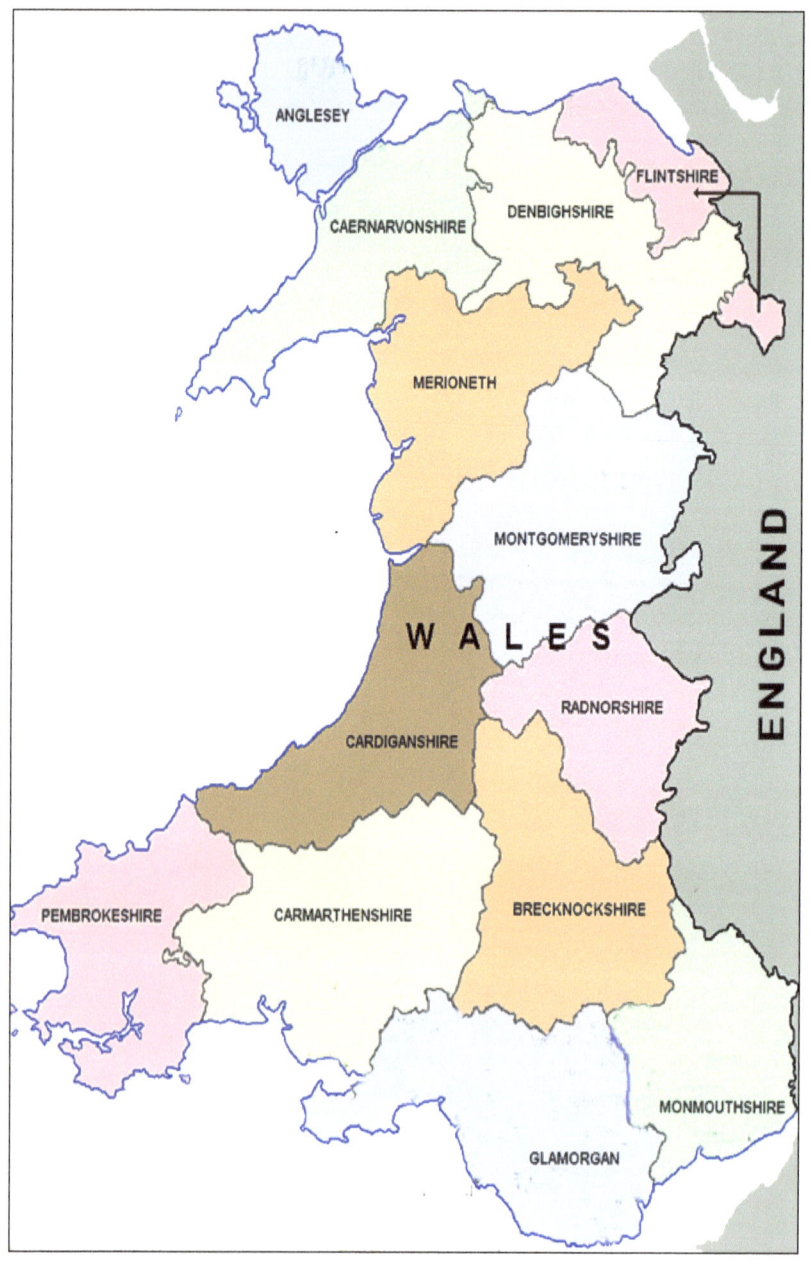

PRESERVED WELSH COUNTIES (2022)

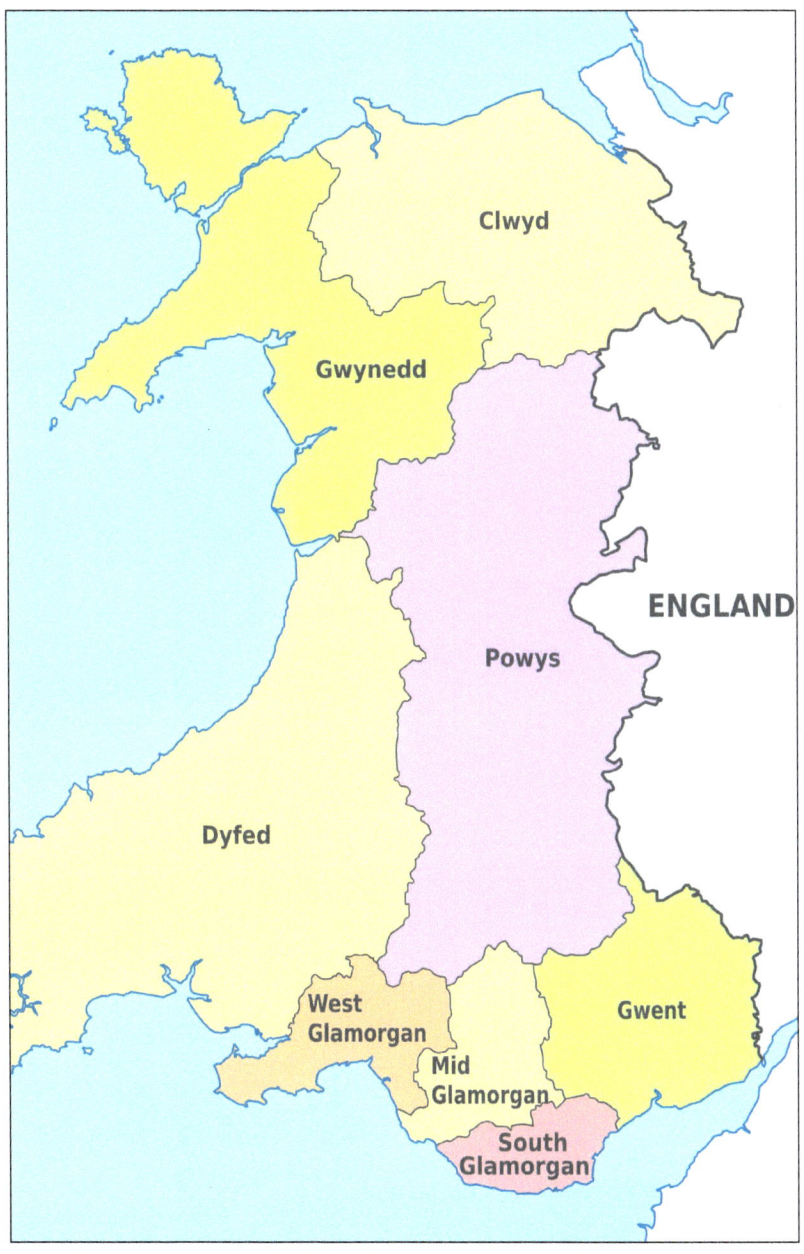

RAIL NETWORK (CURRENT)

www.ingramcontent.com/pod-product-compliance
Lightning Source LLC
Chambersburg PA
CBHW041612220426
43669CB00001B/10